THEY KILLED THE
ICE CREAM MAN

THEY KILLED THE ICE CREAM MAN

My search for the truth behind my brother John's murder

GEORGE LARMOUR

COLOURPOINT

"One of the roles of the arts in a damaged society is to remember the victims. One of the most moving things that ever happened to me was when I wrote the poem 'The Ice-Cream Man'. I got a very affecting letter from his mother. Under her name she printed 'the ice cream man's mother'.

I treasure that letter. She died after he was murdered. I think she died from a broken heart. Letters like that mean far more to me than a hundred good critical notices."

Michael Longley (Poet)

"George's story will resonate with many victims who feel let down and abandoned, having to seek the truth surrounding their loved one's murder themselves. The protection of senior political figures and other officials, has meant that for many 'truth & justice' has had to be forfeited.

However many family members like George, have taken the search for truth into their own hands. I encourage victims to tell their stories publicly, don't let them be forgotten or re-written. If we don't speak up for our dead, who else will?"

Ann Travers (Victims' Campaigner)

"I have been touched by the many stories I heard in the making of my 'Silent Testimony' exhibition. I visited Barnam's, more times than I can remember, with my sister.

Michael Longley's poem 'The Ice-Cream Man' is a favourite of mine. It seems to sum up the fact that the thousands of victims' stories are at risk of being forgotten. That is also the story of 'Silent Testimony'.

Your own story, George, serves as a reminder to us all."

Colin Davidson (Artist)

"George Larmour was forced by circumstance to become an investigator and a journalist after the murder of his brother and the obfuscation around it.

The result is one of the most important books to have come out of the Troubles period."

Malachi O'Doherty (Journalist/Author)

About the Author

George Larmour was born in 1949 and grew up roaming the back streets of the Shankill Road in Belfast. Childhood years that still hold wonderful schoolboy memories, turned into adult years that taught him the harsh realities of life and death.

He spent most of his married life in Bangor, on the North Down coast, with his wife Sadie raising their two daughters.

Working life included sales and managerial positions within the Advertising Department of the *Belfast Telegraph* and he was a member of the original management team that launched Belfast Community Radio, now Q Radio.

In the 1980's he published a monthly entertainment magazine called *Night Life*. This was his modest contribution to helping create a degree of optimism in the midst of the mayhem of those dark years of the Northern Ireland "Troubles" when happiness and night life was in short supply, particularly in Belfast.

George also went on to register the name 'Danny Boy' as an official trademark. He produced a range of Danny Boy branded giftware that he sold throughout Ireland and worldwide via the Internet before selling off the company and trademark to local business entrepreneur and lottery winner, Peter Lavery who has gone on to successfully launch a unique, award winning Danny Boy Irish Whiskey brand.

Now retired, George spends his time writing and telling his young grandsons stories of great, fantastical adventures that bring smiles to their innocent young faces that remind him of his own days of innocence on the Shankill Road all those years ago before the "Troubles" changed so many lives forever.

They Killed the Ice Cream Man is his first book.

(Photograph courtesy of Malachi O'Doherty)

Published 2016 by Colourpoint Books
an imprint of Colourpoint Creative Ltd
Colourpoint House, Jubilee Business Park
21 Jubilee Road, Newtownards, BT23 4YH
Tel: 028 9182 6339
Fax: 028 9182 1900
E-mail: sales@colourpoint.co.uk
Web: www.colourpoint.co.uk

First Edition
First Impression

A catalogue record for this book is available from the British Library.

Designed by April Sky Design, Newtownards
Tel: 028 9182 7195
Web: www.aprilsky.co.uk

Printed by W&G Baird, Antrim

ISBN 978-1-78073-104-9

Front cover: (*main*) Barnam's World of Ice Cream on the night of John Larmour's murder.
(*Pacemaker Press*)

Rear cover: (*top*) George Larmour (*Courtesy of Malachi O'Doherty*),
(*middle*) Malachi O'Doherty (*Courtesy of Malachi O'Doherty*),
(*bottom*) Michael Longley (*Courtesy of Colin Davidson*).

Contents

Dedication 9

Foreword. 11

Chapter One: 11 October 1988 15

Chapter Two: The Search for the Truth 21

Chapter Three: Viva Espana: October 1988 23

Chapter Four: The Cold Reality of Death 27

Chapter Five: A Call from Jack 32

Chapter Six: One Year Later: October 1989 36

Chapter Seven: A Typical Big Belfast Family 41

Chapter Eight: Hunting and Shooting. 47

Chapter Nine: Opening the Parlour Again 49

Chapter Ten: The Gibraltar Three: March 1988 58

Chapter Eleven: Milltown Cemetery 60

Chapter Twelve: Left-Footers. 62

Chapter Thirteen: Dunkirk: 1940. 64

Chapter Fourteen: The Envelope 66

Chapter Fifteen: Waterstones Bookshop: 1999 71

Chapter Sixteen: Remembering Mr Hasty: 1974 76

Chapter Seventeen: Meeting Mrs Hasty: 2005 80

Chapter Eighteen: Unfinished Business: October 2002. 85

Chapter Nineteen: Blair's Weasel Words. 88

Chapter Twenty: The Browning 9 mm. 93

Chapter Twenty-One: Destroying Evidence 96

Chapter Twenty-Two: The Speed Six Ruger. 100

Chapter Twenty-Three: Protecting the Past 102

Chapter Twenty-Four: Eames/Bradley. 105

Chapter Twenty-Five: The Search for DNA 107

Chapter Twenty-Six: The Ruger Serial Number 112

Chapter Twenty-Seven: The Ruger Report 116

Chapter Twenty-Eight: Drawing My Own Conclusions 119

Chapter Twenty-Nine: Ronald Reagan's Rugers. 124

Chapter Thirty: A Close Encounter 128

Chapter Thirty-One: "I was never in the IRA". 132

Chapter Thirty-Two: Channel 7 Australia. 136

Chapter Thirty-Three: Sunday Sequence. 139

Chapter Thirty-Four: The Usual Suspects. 142

Chapter Thirty-Five: Double Standards. 149

Chapter Thirty-Six: Super Tout. 152

Chapter Thirty-Seven: Dear Mr Baggott – Again 156

Chapter Thirty-Eight: Passing the Buck 160

Chapter Thirty-Nine: The Silencing of a Lawyer 164

Chapter Forty: The Estate Agent. 169

Chapter Forty-One: The Police Ombudsman. 175

Chapter Forty-Two: A Question of Truth 180

Chapter Forty-Three: Turning Another Page 185

Epilogue 193

Acknowledgements. 195

Index. 196

Dedication

I dedicate this story to my wife, Sadie and our daughters, Alison and Emma, who allowed me the space and time to put my thoughts on paper and who have put up with my grumpiness over too many years; also to Jack and Charlie for letting me know every day, with arms out wide, that they love Granny and me "this much".

To my mum and dad, who died prematurely from broken hearts, despite what their death certificates indicate; and my sister Jean, who was always there for me during the dark days.

To John McCann, for saving my dad at Dunkirk and being a true friend for the rest of his life.

To Michael Longley, for penning "The Ice-Cream Man" – thank you for ensuring that my brother John would not be just another statistic of our so-called "Troubles", easily forgotten like too many others.

To all the other victims of our grubby sectarian conflict and their families, who deserve the truth. Your own stories deserve to be told and your voices to be heard.

To Mr Jimmy Hasty, and his wife Margaret and family. Holding you as you died on that cold pavement changed my life forever, Mr Hasty. I will never forget you.

To all my friends and work colleagues over all the years – too many to name. But Sean, Sam, Billy and Mike, we had some good times; big Brian in Scotland, keep enjoying the Bush; Fred and Willy John, I still miss you, old pals.

And of course to the memory of my brother John. In telling my story, John, I hope I have helped show that your death should never have happened, and that those who sanctioned it, carried it out and covered up the truth should hang their heads in shame.

George Larmour

*To the living we owe respect, but to
the dead we owe only the truth.*

Voltaire

Foreword

My name is George Larmour. I was born in March 1949 in Belfast, Northern Ireland, at 35 Northumberland Street. That little terraced house – with its miserably cold outside toilet and tin bath on the hook in the whitewashed back yard – has long gone, but the street is still there. It runs between the Shankill Road and the Falls Road.

Those childhood days are history, but the memories remain. We got to lie in on Sunday mornings, my brother John and I, and to have breakfast in bed. Such working-class luxury! It was Dad's job every week to prepare a big fry and when we heard him make his way down the creaking stairs, we knew it was time.

We would lie there, waiting for the aroma to waft upstairs, like some marinated ghost. It took Dad ages, but it was worth the wait. It was the whole works: a slice of thick crispy bacon; a juicy overweight sausage, bursting out of its skin; a fried egg – or sometimes two, if he was still hung over; triangles of soda and potato bread with lashings of tomato sauce. A future heart attack on a plate, but heaven at the time. It's funny how your brain can store away a smell or a taste. Just thinking about those breakfasts brings all the flavours and aromas back to me.

My childhood days were spent mostly "up the road", in Woodvale Park. Like most kids with over-active imaginations, encouraged by regular celluloid adventures at the local cinemas – the Stadium, the Crum or Wee Joe's – our favourite game was Cowboys and Indians, and stalking each other in the bushes. For some reason, I was always chosen to be the Indian Chief – never Billy the Kid or Kemo Sabe, the Lone Ranger, or his faithful sidekick, Tonto.

I, Big Chief Crazy Horse, would watch from my chosen hiding place as, week after week my mates, those fearless cowboys, would gallop towards me across the prairie, slapping their arses to make their imaginary horses go faster, oblivious to the danger that awaited them. Like all ruthless killers, I knew that a carefully planned ambush was the best way to add another scalp to a trophy belt of death. Yeah, if you want to kill someone, an ambush is the best way – they don't see it coming.

We usually ended those Wild West games with a competition to see who could die best – that is, who could die the loudest. Only John Wayne or some stony-faced sheriff could take a bullet without making a sound, but that wasn't real acting in our world. Clutching your chest with a blood-curdling scream – as invisible bullets from a tiny toy six-shooter tore into your jerking body – guaranteed you a chance of being judged as having the best death in our game.

We would eventually go home, exhausted from all these agonising scenes. Sometimes cuts and scrapes added to the adventure but, as often as not, we headed home to our OK Corrals with dirty knees and muddy boots, most likely to face another telling-off from the real chiefs in our houses – our mums.

One lasting memory of those happy times was the occasion on which my big brother John took me to the Falls Baths, when I was about seven. This was the council-operated swimming pool, just down the street and a few hundred yards along the Falls Road. We didn't have our own swimming shorts, but for a penny you could rent a pair of the regulation red V-shaped loincloths that knotted at the side. An early prototype of Speedos for boys, they barely covered a bony backside.

We'd change in one of the wooden cubicles that ran along both sides of the pool. John was a great swimmer and a real daredevil. He thought nothing of climbing the stairs and jumping off the balcony into the deep end. Even away from our prairie park adventures, to my mind, the Indian Chiefs were still close by. This wild flight into six feet of chlorinated and kid-infested water was usually accompanied by a firmly-held nose, and a scream of "Geronimo!" for added effect. One size definitely didn't "fit all" in this instance, and such a mad leap usually guaranteed that your loincloth would end up around your ankles or drifting somewhere across the surface of the pool.

This was a time – in the late 1950s and early 1960s – when Protestant kids from the Shankill Road thought nothing of learning to swim on the Catholic Falls Road.

One day, when my big brother John was busy performing another of his balcony high dives, a regular from the Falls area who looked even younger than I was, managed to haul me to safety, after I went under for a second time, spluttering and coughing in panic. "Keep yer mouth shut or ye'll swalley water – it's fulla piss, ya know," he wisely advised me. Then he confidently and effortlessly swam away underwater to the deep end, where I never dared to venture.

Magical memories, but despite my brother's best efforts and me making sure I never again "swalleyed" water, I never did learn to swim. I was always afraid of the water. Geronimo wouldn't have been impressed. It's too late now – I am almost 66 and a few stone overweight. "Big Chief Sitting Bull" seems a more appropriate name for me these days. And, as for wedging myself into a strained red loincloth, that's an image best left off the page.

Looking back, it is clear that we didn't realise how poor we really were. Times were hard, but we didn't care. We were happy and didn't go hungry. A thick slice of bread, toasted, smothered in butter and sprinkled with sugar or coated with my granny's homemade jam – that was enough for us. And we had each other. Sure, wasn't that all that mattered?

Throughout my life, people have remarked on my simple answer for everything that is wrong in the world or in relation to situations where someone is facing impossible odds. I always respond by saying: "As long as you're happy."

That well-used phrase sums up what, to me, is important in life. And it certainly summed up my innocent childhood, those blackboard years filled with schoolboy adventures. Sadly, as much as I try to hold onto the comforting blanket of these memories, some recollections are fading with age. And others have been deliberately erased, callously ambushed and wiped away by men with an insatiable appetite for evil – to be replaced by a choking shroud of grief and despair.

Since October 1988, I have continued to repeat my saying, "As long as you're happy". But there have been so many times that I wasn't. Everyone has a story to tell. This is mine.

THE ICE-CREAM MAN

Rum and raisin, vanilla, butter-scotch, walnut, peach:
You would rhyme off the flavours. That was before
They murdered the ice-cream man on the Lisburn Road
And you bought carnations to lay outside his shop.
I named for you all the wild flowers of the Burren
I had seen in one day: thyme, valerian, loosestrife,
Meadowsweet, tway blade, crowfoot, ling, angelica,
Herb robert, marjoram, cow parsley, sundew, vetch,
Mountain avens, wood sage, ragged robin, stitchwort,
Yarrow, lady's bedstraw, bindweed, bog pimpernel.

Michael Longley, *Selected Poems*
(Reproduced with permission. Jonathan Cape, 1998)

Chapter One

11 October 1988

"Have ya any chocolate?"

There was no right answer. This man was going to kill him anyway.

I'm sure John cursed quietly to himself for having put the cones away so soon. It wasn't yet closing time – 10.00 pm – but it wasn't far off. Another two minutes and he'd have locked the door and wouldn't have had to serve any more customers that night.

But there the man stood, one more of the many customers who had made their way to stand at the counter that cold October night. This one wanted chocolate. John bent down to get the brittle ice cream cones out of the box.

Opening the ice cream parlour that July had been a quick decision for me and my wife. Choosing the location was no problem. The Lisburn Road in Belfast was probably the busiest for traffic, apart from the city centre itself, and even that was empty at night in those dangerous days. I had sat in my car at different times of the day and night, counting pedestrians and cars passing the boarded-up house. The figures were impressive, no matter what time I made the count. Yes, the Lisburn Road was the ideal spot and the top end was where the money was.

Lots of cars used that road in and out of the city, and within walking distance lay a huge catchment area of housing, where families lived with hordes of children who were sure to love our fantastic ice cream. A bit of work would be needed to turn the ground floor of the vacant house into a vibrant ice-cream parlour, but the decision was made, the lease was signed and the adventure was soon to begin. It was only intended to be a sideline for my wife, Sadie: I already had my own small business, publishing local magazines and advertising-based wall planners.

The name was the difficult part. Should we go for something Italian – like the famous Morelli's in Portrush and Portstewart? Just the name, "Morelli's", meant ice cream to most people in Northern Ireland – those, whose annual summer holiday was a week up the coast in the "Port" – or at the very least, a day trip there. It was worth the risk of backache or whiplash on the dodgem cars in Barry's Amusements, when the day was rounded off with a generous scoop of one of Morelli's famous flavoured ice creams – or a towering, expertly swirled, whipped vanilla cone.

We were not Italian, nor could we pretend to be. Even saying ours would be Italian-style ice cream didn't feel right. We had plans for 21 different flavours, each in a different colour – something unheard of in Belfast at the time. So how to find a name that would do justice to this new world of flavours and colours? It had to be something children couldn't resist, something suggestive of a circus of mystery and wonder. That was when my wife came up with the name – "Barnum's World of Ice Cream". It was perfect! We could already see the delight on the faces of the children and the mums and dads when they would recognise the famous circus name. We changed the spelling to "Barnam's", in case we found ourselves on the wrong end of a copyright lawsuit – then we ordered up the signs and menus.

After a few months of decorating, carpentry work and tiling, the tired old house had been transformed into a bright, modern ice cream parlour. Barnam's opened for business on 12 July 1988. We thought our marketing strategy in this was perfect. Each year on 12 July, thousands of Orange Lodge members, bandsmen and women would march up the Lisburn Road, followed by revellers. The forecast predicted warm sunshine, just the job for Tropical Mango dipped in chocolate sprinkles and topped off with a flake. We'd make a fortune on our first day. It was going to be that easy.

It wasn't, of course. We were right about the thousands of people walking past the parlour and returning later that evening. The weather was even hotter than expected. We could hardly believe how many thousands sang, danced and bounded along the burning pavements.

And they kept on walking – right past our brand new World of Ice Cream. Very few stopped. We were invisible, it seemed. They hadn't heard about our new wonderland of delight. Their taste buds never came close to being tantalised or tingled that day. Not by our ice cream, anyway. The day cost us around £70 in wages and other overheads, and we lifted a pitiful £43. Our enthusiasm quickly melted. But we hoped for better days ahead. They couldn't have been any worse.

Of course we had been noticed. Someone had been watching the new Belfast ice cream parlour. And here he was, on that night in October the same year, asking if Barnam's sold chocolate flavour. A stupid question – of course we did. Barnam's had only been trading for three months, but our reputation had soared, once that disastrous opening was behind us. We'd built up a solid base of customers, who returned again and again to sample our many delights. Each day brought new faces too.

Had he been a regular customer, arriving at two minutes before closing time, he'd have known we sold chocolate flavour. We had flavours to suit all tastes after all, including those traditional flavours that you could see on display in any ice cream parlour in any part of the world. Just what our less adventurous, and more mature, clientele came back for time and again.

But most of our ice creams had more appealing and original names. There was the syrupy Fruits-of-the-Forest flavour that exploded in your mouth. Or Honey Bear – creamy vanilla, swirled through with crunchy pieces of honeycomb which became even more sticky and delicious, the longer they were allowed to settle in the mix. Or Rubble Bubble, filled with pieces of real, chewy bubble gum. Anything that mums hated was sure to be a winner with their kids. It took a few weeks for parents to catch on to what was really in Rubble Bubble, and when they did, they hated the idea of their children ending up with a mouthful of bubble-blowing gum. So their kids went for it even more!

The same went for anything with the word "surprise" attached to it – so it was no surprise that we sold a lot of Blue Surprise, an ice cream sea of blue creaminess, laced with thick, gooey extra-navy streaks. Delicious and guaranteed to disgust their parents, it was naturally just what the local runny-nosed kids, especially the boys, wanted to spend their pocket money on. The only thing better was a twin cone of Rubble Bubble *and* Blue Surprise.

Belfast people always did love their ice cream. And our new parlour, Barnam's, with its bright fluorescent, American-style décor and row upon row of frozen delights, quickly caught the attention and imagination of ice cream lovers of all ages.

But this man wasn't a regular. His was a new face. Standing at the counter now, he had left it to the last minute, just narrowly avoiding being locked out and being forced to go without his planned chocolate hit that night.

As he stood there in front of John, he asked if we sold "sliders" – the Belfast name for a thick wedge of ice cream held between two flat wafers. No doubt the name came from the way the wafers can slip and slide across the wedge of ice cream, as you hold it gently between thumb and fingers. The favoured way of eating a slider is to lick your way around all four edges, before finishing off the last of the wafers and the remnants of the dripping ice cream. Cones are certainly less hassle to make and easier to handle.

The new face wasn't alone: he was with a friend, who had stopped at the door, just inside the parlour. Instead of walking up to the counter to check out the ice creams on display, this friend stood guard beside the electricity meter box on the wall beside the door.

When John told the newcomer that we didn't sell sliders, just cones, his response was to casually say "OK", and shrug his shoulders. His friend, the doorman, didn't say anything. He didn't move from his chosen spot; his concentration seemed to be focused on the darkness of the street outside, visible through the sparkling shopfront window, streak-free and wiped clean by John, just ten minutes earlier, of the grubby fingerprints of dozens of happy children. The doorman was watching for any movement, checking the darkness that cloaked the pavement outside; his gloved hand was on the door handle, holding it closed to prevent anyone entering. He was keeping safe the unseen shadow of evil that had arrived in the parlour along with him and his friend at the counter.

The only other customers in the place at the time were two teenagers, seated at a table close to the window. As they finished their ice cream sundaes, they had casually glanced at the two men as they came into the parlour, and looked away again just as quickly. Boyfriend and girlfriend, as regulars they knew that they had only a few minutes left to scrape their dishes clean before Barnam's closed for the night, and they weren't about to waste a morsel of their chosen delights. The silence of the parlour was broken by the sounds of their spoons against the bottoms and sides of their dishes, extracting the last vestiges of hot fudge and strawberry sauce. The two teenagers were oblivious to the invisible shroud of evil that was about to envelop their lives that night.

The man at the counter wasn't a regular, and he didn't know much about the ice cream flavours on offer here in Barnam's. But, as he stood with his arms outstretched, holding the Ruger handgun firmly in both hands, it was clear that he had done this before.

When John straightened up from behind the counter, and, with the crisp cones in his left hand, prepared to scoop generous portions of chocolate ice cream into each one for the new customers, the man leaned over and fired quickly and repeatedly at him, at point-blank range. The sound of the shots shattered the silence. Magnified by the mirrored walls of the parlour, their thunderous explosions drowned out the clinking of spoons, as the two teenagers scraped the final strawberry smears from their glass dishes.

In a reflex attempt at survival, John held the empty cones up in his hand – a futile, fragile shield that couldn't protect him from the four bullets that tore into his body. The first two hit him in the chest, just above and to the left of his heart. Travelling down just a short distance beneath his skin, they exited his body quickly again, causing no life-threatening damage. The third bullet hit his left arm, just below the crease of his elbow, and travelled through his arm and out the other side. Again, no significant damage was done. My brother could easily have survived those wounds.

But as John turned away to his right, trying desperately to avoid the hail of bullets, he was hit by the fourth. Travelling through his left shoulder and then his neck, it destroyed the front of the cushioning disc between the fourth and fifth vertebrae of his spine, shattering the front of those vertebrae and bruising the spinal cord they protected. John's damaged spinal cord instantly swelled beyond repair, filling the confined space between the fourth and seventh vertebrae. Continuing its journey of death, the bullet finally lodged in his right shoulder. Its job was done. The chocolate-loving gunman at the counter had accomplished his task. John's rag-doll body spiralled down to the floor behind the counter, crushing the brittle cones. Raspberry lifeblood seeped from his wounds, pooling around him on the tiled floor.

The man at the door opened the meter box and flicked the main switch, sucking the fluorescent life out of the parlour. It was now his turn to show how courageous he was, as he fumbled awkwardly for cold, hard metal in the warmth of his coat pocket. He could still see the shapes sitting at the table. The two ice cream loving teenagers were just a few feet away, frozen with fear, unable to react. They were no threat to the doorman, who now held his Browning 9 mm in his hand. But he didn't hesitate.

Quickly, he fired eight bullets at the shadowy figures. Each shot created a fiery flash that bounced off the mirrors, briefly lighting up the darkness. Some of the reckless, random bullets gouged splintered holes in the wooden skirting board beside their feet, and deep, powdery craters in the pink plaster walls just above their heads. But three of his bullets found their targets. One tore into the side of the young lad as he threw himself across the table, vainly trying to protect his girlfriend. A second ripped into his shoulder. The third bullet entered his girlfriend's chest, just above her heart.

The gunman who had wanted to know if we had any chocolate ice cream and sliders leaned over the glass counter and fired two more bullets into the darkness of the floor. It was all over; their job was done.

It was now 10.00 pm. Closing time. Those two minutes changed so many lives forever that October night in 1988. Two teenagers had been left badly wounded, their innocence destroyed.

And they had killed the ice cream man.

Chapter Two

The Search for the Truth

In the four hours following John's murder, a total of 22 police and forensics specialists visited Barnam's, including two Chief Superintendents, two Superintendents, a Chief Inspector and four Inspectors. Hardly wise, given the potential for cross-contamination of possible evidence by so many individuals entering a crime scene. However, I anticipated that the rapid deployment of so many specialists and experienced officers would produce equally swift results and convictions.

Two days later, a brief statement from the IRA appeared in the weekly Republican newspaper, *An Phoblacht*. Under the headline, "RUC Man Killed", the sickeningly glib and self-congratulatory article read:

> … Skilful intelligence work enabled the IRA to pinpoint the movements of an RUC man on Tuesday night, 11 October, and kill him. The operation, carried out by two IRA Volunteers armed with handguns, took place at around 10.00 p.m. at Barnam's ice cream parlour on the Lisburn Road in South Belfast. Despite the close proximity of Lisburn Road RUC Barracks, the unit managed to evade a crown forces' follow-up search, and returned safely to base.

Within weeks, ballistics tests on retrieved bullets confirmed the types of weapons used: a Ruger and a Browning. The names of the gunmen were also known to the police. A week later, I found a scrap of paper in John's car – which had not been searched by the team investigating his murder, despite it being parked directly outside Barnam's the night he was killed. On the paper was written the registration number of another vehicle, along with the word "Sierra". I was curious as to why John had felt it important to note this vehicle model and number. Did he notice this car following him to Barnam's that night?

I took the piece of paper to Donegall Pass police station. As one of the detectives began checking the registration number, and the possible owner of the vehicle, another senior detective asked me if I would look at some mugshots. He settled me down at a nearby desk with two very large folders that contained hundreds of black-and-white photographs of people he referred to as "persons of interest". It took me about 30 minutes to look through all the photos, but I eventually picked out two. The senior detective then asked me if I knew either of the two men in the photographs I had selected. I answered that I didn't, but that somehow they looked familiar to me: otherwise I couldn't pinpoint any particular reason why I had chosen them. I suggested that they might have been customers in Barnam's at some stage during the previous few months, but that I couldn't be certain.

To my surprise, at this point the senior detective voluntarily said that one of the people I had selected owned a Ford Sierra whose registration number matched that written on the piece of paper. I was totally dumbfounded. Had John actually noted the car number of a person connected to his murder? Had I just put a face to that person?

Naïvely, I thought then that justice for my brother was only a matter of weeks away. I didn't realise that certain people had their own agenda, which didn't involve bringing his killers to justice. My long search for the truth was just beginning.

Chapter Three

Viva Espana: October 1988

"I haven't been there myself, but I hear it's a favourite with parents of young children: it has its own pool and it's just a short walk to the beach." That was the description our local travel agent in Belfast had given of the hotel complex Duquesa de Espana in Spain. And it was cheap. How could we resist?

Sadie and I weren't looking for luxury. Just a quick week away, anywhere with a bit of sun and some fun for the kids. We really needed a break from the hassle of work, after the intense few months since March, which we had spent getting Barnam's ready for business. The three months since we had opened in July had been even more hectic. So a week away was just what we all needed that October.

It wasn't summertime but maybe, we hoped, the sun would still be shining in Spain. "Sure, doesn't the sun always shine in Spain?" our cheery travel expert had reassured us when we asked that question. Maybe her comment wasn't so much a confirmation of the weather we could expect, but more a question of her own that she didn't really know the answer to.

Anyway, as I said, we needed a break and anywhere would be better than Belfast. We arrived at our destination late in the evening of Friday, 7 October. It was dark, but our first impressions seemed okay. The coach driver was Spanish but we were disappointed when, in broken English, he welcomed us to Spain and told us his name was Albert. He could at least have lied and added some excitement to our cheap holiday, by telling us he was Diego or Manuel. Anything, but plain old Albert! He dropped us off at the reception door, dumped our suitcases on the ground, pointed at the sign and the bell on the wall, and off he went.

The next morning, we awoke with some excitement. However, we soon realised that it wasn't as cold as Belfast – it was bloody colder! And our travel expert's idea of "a short walk" didn't match the half-hour trek we had to make to get to the nearest beach. Fortunately though, the kids loved the pool at the hotel, despite the lack of heat. So we did our best to enjoy the trip and make the most of our well-earned holiday. Lying reading a book on the inappropriately named "sun loungers", as our young daughters splashed away to their hearts' content, seemed idyllic compared to the daily hassle we would be facing back in Belfast, with hordes of snotty-nosed kids pestering us in Barnam's.

It was mid-morning on Wednesday, 12 October. As we were making our way to the stairs to go up to our rooms, we inspected ourselves in the oversized mirror in the reception area, to see how our tans were coming along. They weren't. Our colouring was more of a healthy, all-over flush from the short dips we had managed to brave so far in the unheated pool. Suddenly I heard someone call out my name.

"¡Hola! Mr Lamar – message, please!" The man at reception was waving a piece of paper at me. "Fone home soonest" was scrawled across the piece of paper. The receptionist sensed my confusion. "You," he pointed at me. He put his fist to his ear. "Phone."

"I have to phone home?" I asked

"Si," he replied. He looked pleased that he had managed to impart the important message, but concerned about what it might mean. I knew exactly what it meant. I have no idea how, but at that precise moment, I knew my brother was dead.

From the hotel reception, I telephoned my mum back in Belfast. The phone rang just twice before I heard my sister's voice. "Mummy, it's George," I heard her say as she passed the phone to my mother.

"Are you coming home, son?" Mum asked me at once.

I didn't need to ask, but I did anyway. "What's happened?"

"The IRA shot John last night."

I didn't need to ask where, but I did anyway.

"In the parlour, in Barnam's," she said, her voice beginning to crack.

Although again I knew the answer, I asked the question anyway.

"Is he dead?"

"He is, son. Are you coming home?"

"Yes, I'll be home as soon as I can. Anyone else hurt?" I asked.

"Yes – two customers."

"Are they okay?"

"I think so."

"Right Mum, I have to go but I'll get home soon."

"Please do, son, please do."

I put the phone down. My wife stood staring at me as she held our young daughters' hands. She had worked out enough from the one-sided telephone conversation to know that something was seriously wrong.

"What's happened – has your dad crashed the car?" Sadie asked at once. We had left our car behind for my father to use while we were away. Sadie had already said it might be too big for him to drive.

"No, it's not Dad. It's John. The IRA shot him in Barnam's last night. He's dead." I reached to grab her as I saw her slump back against the wall and her legs start to buckle. Her scream is something I will never forget. It seemed to go on forever in the stillness of the hotel lobby. The guy on reception just stared at me and the look of recognition on his face said it all.

I contacted the local travel courier and hurriedly got us packed to go home. Our five-year-old was still asking why we couldn't go back to the pool when the car arrived to take us to the airport. The innocence of childhood!

There were no flights leaving for Belfast that day. We managed however to get seats on a flight to London Heathrow, with a connecting flight from Gatwick to Belfast, courtesy of British Airways – a £1,200 dent in my credit card.

As the plane taxied to its allotted runway, the cabin crew handed out free UK newspapers. There was no escaping the claustrophobic wave of grief that rolled over us, as we watched row upon row of untanned tourists scan the front page headlines and turn the pages to read inside the detailed news reports on my brother's murder. According to these articles, at the request of the RUC back in Belfast, Interpol was frantically searching Spain for the murdered officer's brother, who was holidaying there with his family. They had been asked to locate me and notify me of John's murder, and arrange for our immediate return home.

I never did get a call from an Interpol agent. Sadly, the world's largest international police organisation, presumably with access to border passport control intelligence, proved woefully inept at finding an ordinary family of four soaking up the rain in Spain. Hopefully they're having more success with some of the names on their "Most Wanted" list.

When we finally arrived at Heathrow, we were tired and, even with a hectic dash, it looked as if we were going to miss our connecting Gatwick flight to Belfast. Somehow however, British Airways ground staff were now aware of our arrival, and a very pleasant and caring lady had us whisked across to Gatwick and straight onto the plane.

Inevitably, when we saw them, my mum and dad looked utterly distraught, overcome with unbearable heartache. They were glad I was home, but nothing I said could ease their sorrow. I went to the funeral parlour and stood close to my big brother. I felt very lonely.

Chapter Four

The Cold Reality of Death

When my wife and I opened Barnam's World of Ice Cream, we wanted to be sure to make it a happy experience for customers, and particularly the children from the local area. It wasn't just about selling ice cream. It was about the smiles on the faces of those children, as they surveyed the 21 flavours on display. They had never seen so many kinds of ice cream in one shop before. So in that sense, for us, Barnam's was a success from the very beginning.

Despite my marketing expertise however, there was one event that October that I had no experience in organising. I didn't need to arrange for any comedians or clowns or specially printed T-shirts or catchy advertisements for this one. I had no prior knowledge of how to arrange a funeral.

Until that point, my only experience of death up close had been when I was about 13, and I saw an old man who lived down the street, lying dead in his coffin. There had been people coming and going all day at his house, paying their respects. The curiosity of a young teenager was what made me go in. No one stopped me looking, as I peeked through the gaps between the people standing around in the room. There he was! He looked scary, and it's an image I have never forgotten.

I don't know what was more traumatic for me at that young age – the sight I had just witnessed, of the old man lying in his coffin, or the words I heard one of the mourners say, which made everyone laugh. It seemed somehow wrong to me that people were laughing at such a sad time.

This mourner was about 70 years old, and looked like she wouldn't be too far behind joining the company of the deceased in the corner. Half-filled tumbler of stout in hand – no doubt one of many that night – she was impressing upon the female friend who was with her, as well as the rest of the room, what her own final wishes were for the time when she "kicked the bucket", as she referred to her last physical act in this life.

She was adamant that she didn't want the local undertaker to take care of her funeral. She'd heard stories about perverted undertakers taking a quick peek at women during the wee small hours. Nodding her head downwards, she exclaimed, "I don't want that wee skitter up the road to be looking at my bits down there in the middle of the night! The wee frigger. God, I'd rather die than have that wee shite see my bare arse and my thingamajig, so ah would."

I'd only just entered my spotty, pubescent teens, but even I knew enough about sexual attraction to know that it was highly unlikely that the "wee skitter" funeral director would have been in the least interested in her "thingamajig" down there anyway. She was a big, hefty housewife. More like a man than a woman. She had arms that looked like she would be able to hug you so tight, you would gladly surrender and beg for release. And she had a hairy top lip that seemed to crawl like a caterpillar when she talked.

Many years had passed since I saw the old man looking very dead in his coffin, with his shirt collar hanging on his frail neck. During that time, I had made sure not to look at another dead body. I even refused to look at my Granny in her coffin when she died. I didn't want the same sort of memories and images filling my dreams – I wanted to remember her as she was. As the years passed, I often wished I had looked at her body. I missed her, and not seeing her that last time had somehow left a strange emptiness in my life that is hard to explain.

And now here was my brother John, lying in a box in a drab room in a funeral parlour, looking surprisingly peaceful. He wasn't like that old man. He was still young and healthy-looking, with a holiday glow – courtesy of some carefully applied make-up. His shirt and coat fitted perfectly, and his tie was knotted just the way he had always done it himself. I kept looking at his face, trying to remember how it moved when he talked and laughed, and when he was angry. I'd never seen him look so still, so quiet.

I remember, when I was about four or five, how my dad would let me sit and brush his hair. I would get Mum's big hairbrush, and he would sit in the chair and let me create different styles. He would always pretend to fall asleep. Meanwhile I would be smiling over at Mum, and she would nod and egg me on. I'd make sure his hair was sticking up like a hedgehog. He'd then waken from his pretend sleep, look in the mirror and chase me around the room, looking like not only the last, but the only Mohican in Belfast.

But my brother wasn't going to wake up now, like my dad used to do. Nothing I could do to his hair that night would change the situation. This wasn't a pretend sleep. He wouldn't look in the mirror and blame me for the wisp of hair that was lying awkwardly against his forehead.

I ran my hand through his hair and fixed it just the way I remembered it always being. "That'll have to do, John – I never would have been any good as a barber!" I joked as I instinctively touched his cheek. The hardness and coldness of the skin on his face sent a shock through me. I shouldn't have done it – I shouldn't have touched his face. The reality of his death hit me. It took my breath away. That frozen memory is embalmed within me, and it won't go away.

§

I hate funerals. I know, what a stupid thing to say! I'm hardly unique in that regard. I suppose everyone hates funerals. Not exactly a day for celebration – unless the deceased is an ex-husband or wife you had wished dead before the divorce, or you happen to be a funeral director or florist, in which case you look forward to an endless procession of the dead.

I hate the commercialisation of death, the intricate floral designs spelling "Granda", or the deceased's name, or arranged to recreate the crest of his or her favourite football or hockey team. I see no point in the extensive range of splendid oak coffins to choose from, each one varnished to perfection, with matching shiny fake brass handles and a range of satin linings to suit all tastes. It seems such a waste that some people only get to lie on silk when they're dead.

A glossy catalogue displaying the latest, "must-have" designer accessories for the deceased has one sole aim: to get you to spend as much of your cash as possible on your dearly departed's final journey to God knows where. It invites you to provide a public display that you care more about your mum or your dad or close relative than your neighbour does, or did, for theirs. We are expected to keep up with the Joneses, even in death. I often wonder who the Joneses keep up with.

That's just me. Truthfully? I don't really hate funerals. I just want it all to be over as quickly as possible. I cry too easily; I need to. But men don't do that in public, do they? So the longer a funeral goes on, the more difficult I find it all.

I was glad the organising of John's funeral was something I didn't have to be involved with. It was out of my hands. It was to be a formal police funeral, so his colleagues took care of all the preparations. I'd managed to stay strong most of that week, and also during the morning of his burial. My grief was a private affair, kept well out of sight. I had brief, tearful bouts in bathrooms and bedrooms. I was okay in public, until someone hugged me without warning me first. Their well-meaning embrace, intended to make me feel loved, just made me feel more vulnerable. It was in the middle of those well-meaning, comforting hugs that I would feel myself on the cliff edge of grief, almost falling into the abyss.

I was determined to get through the day of the funeral without breaking down. I put on my professional, dignified face for the rest of my family and for the cameras and media I knew would be there. I didn't want John's killers getting the additional satisfaction of seeing me cry – I was determined to show the bastards they hadn't won. Of course, I knew it wouldn't last. I knew that sometime that day, my protective shell would finally fracture and there would be no hiding my pain. Just as long as it wasn't captured on local news footage – that was all that mattered to me.

There were two things that day which almost brought on the tears. The first happened when the minister was performing the private service in the house, before the undertakers carried John's coffin out to the street. As the Reverend Sam McClintock spoke, and a silence fell over the house and the street, John's old black Labrador dog, Sam, began to howl. A low, painful cry that summed up the pain of all of us. I found it hard not to join Sam in his public display of grief. He needed someone to tell him everything was okay. Eventually, one of the mourners led Sam away and tried to comfort him. But the bond between master and best friend was too strong. He knew it wasn't okay.

Later, as John's funeral procession neared the end of the road, the sounds of a rugby match drifted across from the nearby school playing fields. Then suddenly they stopped, as if someone had just abruptly turned off a radio commentary. We watched in silence, as both teams of muddy teenagers formed two lines on the pitch and stood with their heads bowed. A simple gesture of respect for someone they didn't know, which for me almost brought on the dreaded flood of public tears.

There were lots of people at John's funeral that day: most of them, I didn't know. Many said their polite farewells at the church or in the cemetery, but dozens came back to the house for the regulation cup of tea and sandwiches, or glass of what they fancied, to send John on his final journey. That one-way trip we will all have to make one day.

Of these neighbours, police colleagues, drinking pals, distant cousins, some had the courage to say something funny and make us all laugh. Most however looked genuinely heartbroken. Have you ever noticed how most people at funerals always say the same things? And they can't just say their piece and leave it at that. They always feel compelled to prove how genuine they are, by leaning forward and holding your hand and whispering it to you. As if afraid they might wake the dead if they raise their voice. "Sorry for your trouble." "He's in a better place now."

"God only takes the good ones." I don't know who he was. He probably knew that I was the brother, and he approached me as I was taking a stroll up the street on my own. I had needed to get away from all the suffocating sorrow that was smothering me in that house.

It was out of me before I had time to think and I forgot to lean forward, hold his hand and whisper it. "Does, he now? Well, f**k that! It's about time he took a few of the bad bastards, if you ask me."

He stared back at me in disbelief. As I walked away, I heard him mumble something about there being no need for that sort of language on a day like this, and with my brother still warm in his grave.

Whoever he was, he didn't deserve my anger. There was no need for me to take it out on him. I briefly turned and said I was sorry. The dam of tears that I had kept stored away burst through and dissolved my protective shell. He was right – there wasn't any need for that sort of language on a day like this. But he was wrong about John – he wasn't "still warm in his grave". God. He definitely wasn't warm.

I kept walking. The tears wouldn't stop.

Chapter Five

A Call from Jack

Christmas 1988 certainly wasn't a time for the usual festive celebrations in our family. The last thing any of us felt interested in was the festive season: we were dreading it, in fact. As for me, what was left of that fateful October, November and December had passed in an anaesthetic haze and a self-induced liquid numbness, viewed too often through the bottom of an empty glass of bourbon. Despite its name and its promise, it didn't bring any lasting comfort.

It was such a difficult time. Christmas week arrived. Life around us didn't stop, of course; other people moved on with their lives. For many families in our position however, there didn't seem much point in it all. Seeing people scurrying from shop to shop, loading up with last-minute gifts that probably wouldn't be appreciated much anyway, seemed only to reinforce what was really important in life: life itself, and those we missed. New thick, woollen socks or comfy slippers wouldn't cushion the blow or soften the pain.

On Christmas Eve, the telephone in my brother's house rang. My wife Sadie and I had decided that, with our two daughters, we would spend Christmas with my brother's widow. That was the word the newspapers and television reports kept using when referring to her: "widow". Even saying it now conjures up an image of an old woman in a black mourning shawl. She was his second wife, and younger than him – she seemed much too young to be called a widow.

The telephone call that evening was just one of many that day. We had had a series of often brief calls from people, who wanted to see how we were or just wanted to let us know they were thinking about us. Well-meaning and well-intentioned, of course, but they were becoming tiresome. We did appreciate that there were some people who were genuinely concerned about how we were coping. Other calls however seemed more like they were being made out of a sense of obligation, something the callers knew they should do, but about which they felt uncomfortable and awkward. I'm sure some of these people hung up, feeling that now they had done their duty, they could continue with their celebrations without feeling too guilty at being so happy.

When the phone rang this time, I decided I would answer it. It was well after 9.00 pm, and we were tired. I didn't recognise the voice. The caller seemed to stumble on hearing my male voice. He asked me who I was. When I told him my name was George Larmour, he asked if I was Constable Larmour's brother. He sounded very official.

When I confirmed that I was indeed John's brother, the caller said he was Jack Hermon and, sensing my confusion, elaborated by saying "Chief Constable John Hermon". He said how deeply sorry and genuinely saddened he was about John having been killed. He continued to speak glowingly about him, and reiterated the extent to which the loss of an officer was felt by all the members of the Force. He said the RUC wasn't just a collection of officers – rather, it was one big family and each one felt the pain of the loss of a fellow officer as if it was his or her own brother or sister. He said once more that his own thoughts were with us at that sad Christmas time.

I thanked him for his kind words and asked if he wished to speak to John's wife. He replied that he did, and that that was indeed his reason for calling. So I handed the telephone to my sister-in-law and, covering the mouthpiece, I whispered that it was the Chief Constable, John Hermon. I then listened to the one-way conversation, trying to decipher what he might be saying to her. It was obvious that he was repeating all the kind words I had heard from him during my brief chat with him.

I didn't envy Sir John Hermon the difficult task he felt honour-bound to perform that Christmas Eve. I'm sure – just like the personal visits he had to make to the families of his dead officers, and the many funerals he had to attend – he probably dreaded these emotional, festive season telephone calls.

I don't know how many widows and family members of dead officers the Chief Constable had to telephone that night. Since 1980, during the eight years he had been in charge of the RUC, over 100 RUC officers had been killed. I found myself wondering if he telephoned the same families every year, adding the newly bereaved ones to the list each time. Or did he only telephone a family or widow the year their loved one had been killed, and not repeat the same calls to the same families, year after year? It would take surely too long, if each year he had to speak to each one of the families who had been bereaved during his tenure. The list was getting longer all the time.

As I was reflecting on how many calls Sir John Hermon had to make, I was aware that the call seemed to have come to an abrupt end, with my sister-in-law saying there was no need for an apology; that it was okay and didn't matter. I found myself wondering what Sir John Hermon had to apologise for. My brother's wife, who was supposed to be receiving a telephone call of support from the head of the RUC "family", now appeared to be doing her best to console the most powerful man in the Force.

I have no doubt Sir John made every single call that Christmas Eve to the families of his murdered officers with real sincerity, and that their circumstances caused him personal sadness. But I also have no doubt that this particular year, someone within his administration staff would receive a telephone call from him that wouldn't be so calm and compassionate. For in this instance, someone – the person whose job it was to provide him with the list of family names, telephone numbers and incident details for his important calls – had overlooked one vital detail. This person had made Sir John Hermon look very bad that night.

As soon as my sister-in-law put the phone down, I asked her why the call had ended the way it did. She just laughed, and said that the Chief Constable had asked if she worked herself. Even I laughed when I heard that.

"Really, Sir John Hermon asked you if you worked?" I kept repeating the question, not quite believing what I was hearing.

"Yep, after telling me how sad he was to hear about my husband's murder, and that the RUC family of officers were thinking about me, he asked me if I worked myself."

"And you said . . ?" I asked in utter amazement

"I told him that, yes, I did work. Then I said: 'Sir, I work for you – I am a police officer!'"

John Hermon was the longest-serving Chief Constable of the RUC during the Troubles; he had steered his way courageously through many political and security minefields during the tempestuous violence of 1980s Northern Ireland. But I'm sure that telephone call, on Christmas Eve 1988, caused him greater anxiety and heartache than many of his public duels with even the harshest of his opponents and critics. He certainly didn't deserve the embarrassing situation he found himself in – perhaps because of a simple administration error, or a lapse in concentration on the part of one of his staff. How many of us have said the wrong thing, when trying to comfort someone who has just lost a loved one? Once more, I wondered how many times the Chief Constable had to carry out his dreadful duty that night.

I never spoke to Sir John Hermon again, or got the chance to meet him. I often wanted to tell him not to feel too bad about what happened – and that his embarrassing Christmas Eve telephone call in the midst of our unbearable grief had actually managed to make us laugh out loud. Although he likely didn't realise it, he brought some brief but much appreciated festive cheer into our lives that bleak winter's night in 1988.

One day in 2008, not long after Sir John died, I recognised his wife, Lady Sylvia Hermon, strolling in Donaghadee. She and her family had publicly stated, in the County Down Spectator, that he had died in what they described as, "a long and valiant struggle against the ravages of Alzheimer's" in his final years. So I briefly stopped her that day in Donaghadee, and offered my condolences. Lady Sylvia thanked me for my kind words and asked me if I had worked in the RUC. She must have wondered why I smiled and answered, "No, but I knew someone who did." I didn't elaborate any more at the time, but an image of a – hopefully – laughing Jack Hermon finally enjoying the joke flashed through my mind at that moment.

Chapter Six

One Year Later: October 1989

A hospital ward in the middle of the night is a lonely place. Fading shadows drape the walls. A solitary nurse goes about her duties silently, retracing the same steps across the polished floor again and again. The last regular visitors have long gone, the sounds of their encouraging words and laughter replaced by the muffled, choking coughs of the loved ones left behind on the ward, alone now with their fears and their uncertainties. On the small table beside each patient is an unlit bedside lamp, its long, angled neck closed up for another night, its head peering down like a hooded vulture waiting patiently for its next victim. A warm, sweaty smell of sickness is circulated around the ward by an air-conditioning fan, which itself sounds weary and defeated.

It had been nearly a year since my brother John was murdered, and now here I was, watching death take another close family member – creeping, slowly this time, across a hospital bed. At first, I had willed my father to live. I don't often pray. But I had even tried that, desperate that he should have some happier times after the last twelve months of pain; wishing that I had one last chance to tell him all the things I had never said. But now, as his life and my hopes slowly ebbed away, I wished most of all that his pain would end.

This wasn't the last memory I wanted to have of the man who in his youth had been rescued from the cold, heartless sea-of-defeat off the coast of Dunkirk; the man who went on to courageously fight the Japanese, and malaria, in the jungles of Burma; the man who had wiped away my childhood tears, who could always make it better when I scraped my knee; the man who had promised he would always be there when I needed him, who would always catch me when I fell.

As soon as those distant childhood days tumbled through my mind, I was remembering "Ach-a-knee", when I was small enough to play it. My father would sit me on the edge of his closed knees and sway me from side to side, while he recited the old rhyme:

Ach-a-knee, when I was wee,
I used to sit on my daddy's knee,
Then one day he let me . . .

I always knew what would happen next – that was the best part. There would be a long, deathly quiet pause, and I would hold my breath in anticipation. Then suddenly my father would open his knees and shout, "Fall!" – and I would plunge down the gap, giggling and breathless. A mere two-foot fall of fear and excitement, but one that seemed to last a lifetime. Of course, I knew he would always catch me before I hit the floor, and straight away I would beg him once more: "Do 'Ach-a-knee' again, Daddy!"

Now, as I sat beside his bed, his hands looked so small and frail. With its scrapes and dents, his wedding ring reflected the years, too loose to stay on his finger now without the blue tape holding it safely in place. As I scanned the lines of time around his eyes, it was as if each one had a story to tell. Some I would never know about; others were etched deeply in my memory. I now wanted to fit together – before it was too late, before I lost them forever – the pieces of a jigsaw of memories, which had been tossed carelessly into a box somewhere at the back of my mind. I closed my eyes and there they were – those missing pieces of happiness and innocence.

Long past days, filled with the coarse, musty smell of seaside donkeys; the taste of bitter, cloudy limeade mingling with the ice cream so cold that your cheeks collapsed as you tried to suck it skywards through your straw; the sensation of licking your sticky fingers as you worked your way carefully round a Hallowe'en toffee apple; the sight of gigantic chocolate eggs trundling faster and faster down Easter bunny hillsides in their protective silver coats. Holding on with my knees as I balanced high on strong, broad shoulders that bounced and heaved in celebration of another last-minute goal; hearing the crowd clapping and cheering, and adding my own small voice to the sea of sound that got louder with each frantic wave of a mass of scarves . . . louder and louder . . . and louder!

The sound shocked me out my slumber, dragging me back to the present and away from the comfort of my childhood dreams. As each feeble cough failed to bring him the relief he needed, my father's pain was all too evident. How could I fall asleep now, when he needed me most? I held the cup of water to his lips as gently as he had done for me when I was a child.

As I watched him settle again, I cautiously ventured back to my memories.

But I couldn't find the laughter again. Now I could only remember the years when I had all the answers – or at least I thought I did; those teenage years when parents "just don't understand"; those adolescent years when "Ach-a-knee" was just a stupid, childish game, long forgotten. Years when all I saw was a man who drank too much.

In the past year, he had got drunk many times – and he had cried, something I had not witnessed before. I watched him grow old more quickly than I had ever imagined someone could, in that year that could never be forgotten and that changed all our lives forever. That night in October 1988, my dad had simply lost the will to live when he saw my brother dead on a hospital trolley – his eldest son murdered, his young, body lifeless with four bullet holes in it.

The groan of the hospital fan brought me back again to the present, but only briefly. Now I remembered how, a few days before he was rushed to hospital, my father had taken a small wooden box from his bedside drawer. He didn't say anything, but just tilted his head a little, motioning me to take it. I duly took it and opened it, wondering what dark hidden secret lay within. "Ach, no money as usual, Dad," I had joked, trying to lighten the mood.

His Burma Star medal stared proudly up at me, untarnished by the 44 years it had lain there untouched. Beside it was a khaki pouch that looked worn and stained; inside were five small, faded photographs. The edges were frayed; the surfaces criss-crossed with tiny fault lines. These were black-and-white images that had obviously been handled many times, savoured for comfort on lonely nights far away from home. Cherished, carefully preserved keepsakes, which looked as if they might fall apart if they were looked at just one more time.

There was a photograph of a young man standing proudly, in an army uniform; by his side is a beautiful young girl, a smiling bride in her lace wedding dress – my mum and dad, both so much in love with each other and with life, ready for a future of happy times and adventures together. The second photo was of a very small baby girl: my big sister, Jean. Sitting on the edge of a velvet cushion, she looks like she might sway and topple over at any moment. The third picture was of my big brother John as a child, sitting on the windowsill outside our house, wearing a V-neck jumper and short trousers that were handed down to me a few years later.

I scanned the remaining two photographs in anticipation. They looked like they had been soaked in mud and hurriedly cleaned. There was one of a Japanese soldier, young, handsome and strong. Standing in full uniform, he rests his hand on the braided handle of a magnificent sword that glints in the camera's flash. By his side is a beautiful bride, wearing a silk kimono and holding three white orchids. They look so much in love. The final photo was of a small Japanese boy with arms outstretched, longing for the warmth of a father's embrace.

My dad never spoke to me about the war and I never asked. I never understood what he went through, or knew about the sights he had witnessed and the things he had done. An anguished knot of realisation gripped me as I stared at these two last photographs, stained with their owner's dried blood – happy family images frozen in time, which hid the reality of war. That haunting picture of a little Japanese boy, who would never see his father again, had brought back unspoken memories to my father, and tears of regret filled his eyes.

He had been able to survive the memories of war – those which no doubt kept him awake at night – in his own way. Over the years, drink had helped to blur the images of so many dead and injured. But the sight of his own son, dead – killed by another's hand – was one terrible image too many to bear. His spirit left him then; the liquid kind didn't work anymore.

My father's breathing was getting slower. It was not so much breathing, as small, last-ditch gasps of the warm, stale air – each one just enough to keep him alive. The "Get Well Soon" cards were running out of time.

My brother was the first-born son and, in the family tradition of the working class, he was named after my dad. Two John Larmours, referred to as "big John" and "wee John" to avoid confusion. My father had missed "wee John" so much during the past year.

Although he didn't show affection easily, I know he loved me too. I remember him saying those words to me when I was a child, but not once when I was older. It somehow seemed awkward, not the sort of thing you say to a teenager or another adult male. Especially a father to his son. He couldn't say the words. Couldn't put his arms around me and just say, "I'm a man, I'm your dad, you're my son – and I love you." Then again, I had never told him either. It was always left unsaid after a goodbye wave, as if it was obvious and didn't need saying. But it did. Is it something about fathers and their sons which prevents them doing such a sentimental thing, showing such emotion? It's the sort of thing women do more naturally, but not men.

The dimmed light from the ward filtered through the hospital screens surrounding his bed. We were alone in our private, curtained corner; no one would see or hear. I carefully lifted his head and leaned close to his face. "Daddy, it's George. Can you hear me?" His eyelids flickered, and there was a brief, barely audible acknowledgement. As gently as I could, I put my arms around him and held him. I was literally holding his life in my hands. The thought occurred to me that this was probably the last time I would be able to do this. My voice wobbled. "Dad, I really love you," I whispered, hoping no one would hear me. He opened his eyes and nodded. I could feel his weak hands trying desperately to hold on to me. I looked at his face and saw the life in his eyes. Eyes that said unmistakably, "I love you too, son." I said it again: "I love you, Dad". And I didn't care who heard me.

Gently I laid him down on the bed again. Silent tears filled my eyes. Tears that would help wash away my pain, but would never dilute the memories. Tears of sadness mixed with regrets – but most of all, tears of joy. I had held my dad in my arms and told him I loved him. It was something I missed from those innocent childhood days, and it felt good.

He gasped slowly once more, and I could feel myself holding my breath, waiting for him to do it again. There was that long, deathly silent pause of anticipation. The words filled my mind:

When I was wee,

I used to sit on my daddy's knee,

Then one day . . .

Chapter Seven

A Typical Big Belfast Family

It's January 2015. Another new year of challenges and adventures. I turn 66 at the end of March. Where did all those years go? I'm sitting here, staring at my computer keyboard, wondering if I should continue with this story. October 1988 and 1989 have long gone. Some of the slapped-arse cowboys of my childhood have swapped their stallions for BMW horse power. Others became paramilitaries, found out that real bullets guaranteed them first place in the "best way to die" competition, and were posthumously awarded a life-time achievement award for their efforts. I ask myself, who really gives a damn if I finish this story or not? Probably no one. But I'll do it anyway. I need to do it before it's too late.

I just have to briefly visualise my dad in that hospital bed, and the memories and smells come flooding back. They have never gone away. All that week, he'd kept asking me what date it was. Over and over. On the day before he finally died, he'd kept repeating the same question, like someone suffering from short-term memory loss, desperately hoping that when he asked again, the date would have changed. But hospital days grind slowly and in the end, he just wasn't strong enough to finish the race and last out until the date scarred into his brain. It was only 7 October – he wanted it to be 11 October. He was willing himself to stay alive until then. To his mind, that would have been a good day to die.

He got his wish in part, as it turns out. We buried him on 11 October 1989 – that same date my brother had been murdered the year before. At last he was reunited with his eldest son, his heart no longer broken. His twelve slow months of pain were at an end. The final, morphine-coated sands of time had run out. Before they closed his coffin, I tucked some photos into his coat – the one of the little Japanese boy, the one of the Japanese soldier and his bride, and one of my brother.

John had been a "legitimate target", at least he was in the eyes of the gunmen who pulled the triggers in Barnam's World of Ice Cream on that bitter October night. He had proudly worn the uniform of the Royal Ulster Constabulary, a decision that some would say was courageous, but that others – myself included – would call foolhardy and thankless. Nevertheless, it was a decision taken by many other young women and men who believed that evil should not be allowed to win.

This decision on John's part was enough in itself for his IRA killers to justify their actions. He was, in their terms, a "black bastard": their name for any member of the RUC, and a reference to the colour of the uniform they wore. John was the enemy, a temporary roadblock on their blood-splattered road to Irish freedom. A barrier, which was easily dismantled by a frenzied barrage of bullets during a carefully planned ambush at a time when their victim was off-duty, off-guard and unarmed. Less risk that way – they never see it coming.

My dad wasn't a legitimate target. My mum wasn't a legitimate target either. But the gunmen might as well have sought them out too, crept up on them in an unguarded moment, aimed their guns, looked in their bewildered, questioning eyes, and pulled the triggers on them also. For they killed them anyway.

Like any parents who lose a child of no matter what age, mine never got over this sudden, unbearable amputation from their lives. And just like amputees, who say they feel that unbearable, phantom pain from a missing limb years after they have lost it, my mum and dad couldn't touch or hold or soothe the pain of their loss – but they felt the absence deeply within their souls, every day for the rest of their shortened lives.

They and the rest of my family were the people who were left behind to pick up the broken, jagged pieces – sharp shards of a reality that stabbed at the unseen wounds in their hearts and heads, and intensified the pain to unbearable levels. These were lives that were left empty and hollow; lives in which even the brightest of summer days lost colour and intensity. Lives slowly turned off, bit by bit, day by day, by the cruel, unseen dimmer switch of heartbreak.

My mum, Rosetta, always had time for a private prayer. I suppose it was her way of getting through each day. She always said, if you help someone in need, you will be rewarded with contentment in your own life. So she always found time to pray for others. I often wondered what she had done which was so bad that her final reward should be such heartache and such little contentment in this life.

Mum was the only girl in a family of six children. Born on Christmas Day, she was a very special gift and was loved by her five big brothers – Jackie, Bobby, Billy, Hughie and Geordie. A typical big Belfast family, all those years ago. She was called "Etta" by family and friends.

And as in all big Belfast families, particularly at the time, some of the siblings didn't stay in the land of their birth. The black smoke that drifted from the factories and the magnificent new liners that sailed away from the shipyard stirred up in them dreams of far-off places. Some roots weren't sufficiently strong to keep them here; forty shades just weren't enough. So some spread their wings and sought greener pastures.

Uncle Jackie didn't wander to far-off shores. The first of my mother's big brothers to die, he was deeply religious. They called him "The Preacher", as he always had a suitable quote from the Bible on a Saturday for his brothers and sister when he called to see them in Granny's house. He worked in the shipyard but he would indeed have made a good preacher. Or a professional musician – his soulful renditions on his trumpet, accompanied by his wee sister with her wonderful singing voice, filled our little terraced house with musical memories that I still savour to this day.

Jackie went missing one day in 1960, on his way to work in the Harland and Wolff shipyard in Belfast. He suffered from epilepsy, and it was thought he had perhaps had a seizure and wandered off and lost his memory or his way home. He was missing for 11 days before his body was found floating in the River Lagan. The day he went missing was 11 October: the same fateful date which would touch my family in later years.

Uncle Billy, "The Yank", as his brothers and sister called him in later years, was the first to go looking for that elusive extra shade of emerald. Arriving from Belfast, he found that he had the world at his feet in Boston in the exciting, roaring 1920s. America was good to him. He sold printing services across the Eastern states of that new world, and earned enough to retire to Florida. There the boy from the Shankill spent the rest of his life with sunshine on his face.

Uncle Bobby became a soldier and toured the world – a good career move. He raced through the ranks and was awarded an MBE for his outstanding work as a military strategist in the successful movement and deployment of troops during the Korean War. He was lovingly referred to as "The Major" by his sister Etta, my mum – that is the rank he had achieved when he retired to Scotland, where he lived until his death in January 1989.

Big Uncle Hughie, "The Lanky One", was the tall, skinny brother of the family. I still have old sepia photos from my childhood, of me standing beside the tallest Father Christmas I have ever seen, a bewildered look on my face, as I clutch my Santa parcel under my arm. Was I marvelling at how tall Father Christmas really was, and how he had managed to lose so much weight since the previous Christmas? Or was I trying to figure out why, under that long, cotton wool beard, he somehow looked like someone I knew?

He made a great Santa, did Uncle Hughie. He ended up emigrating to Australia with his family, just before the first sparks of mistrust and sectarian hatred ignited the Troubles here in 1969. A £10 assisted-passage offer to a better life Down Under was too tempting. And even though he missed damp old Belfast, it was indeed a better life out there, filled with sunshine and surfing and barbecues on Bondi Beach. Albeit a short one – Hughie had just 11 years of adventure in New South Wales, with all its wonders and colours. I never saw my big, smiling black-and-white Santa again.

Uncle Geordie didn't roam the globe. Belfast was good enough for him. I was named after him, although I hated being called "Geordie", and as a grumpy kid I always ignored anyone who didn't call me by my proper name. He was like a dad to me, along with my own. I was glad he stayed in Belfast. I would have missed his laughter too much.

I don't think Uncle Geordie was given a nickname by his brothers or sister. But I called him "Marvellous". He was widowed many years, but he loved life. He walked everywhere with a stride that would have shamed younger men. He was a supporter of Belfast's worst football team, Cliftonville. In those early days of the 1950s it was a team supported by fans on both sides of the religious divide. It wasn't a case of whether Cliftonville would be beaten on any particular Saturday, but simply by how many goals. Six–nil was the usual story each week, but Uncle Geordie always went along the following Saturday anyway, just in case their form improved. Whenever you spoke to him and told him anything about yourself, he always beamed and answered, "Marvellous!"

In his later years, when he got too old and unsteady to walk anymore, he only wished for one thing in life. "Give me back my youth" was his one simple request. As he grew older, he also had trouble hearing. When he didn't actually hear what you had said, he would just say, "Marvellous!", before you had finished your tale, and you would know to repeat the story and speak louder this time.

After Dad died, Mum and Uncle Geordie lived two doors down from each other in Belfast, each alone in their cosy little pensioner's bungalow. He was missing his wife, Aunt Ella, and Mum was missing wee John and Dad. Brother and sister looked out for each other. The days were long and they both welcomed a phone call or visit from me or my sister, or any other friend or family member. You didn't visit Mum without calling in to see Uncle Geordie as well.

When no one called, they always had each other to break the monotony, with a brief chat or bit of shared supper, or in Uncle Geordie's case, a welcome tot of whiskey to keep the cold away. They had keys to each other's houses. They didn't ring each other's doorbells, but they would have a quick check through the front window before letting themselves in.

Uncle Geordie did that one day in late August 1994 – just a quick look, to see if Mum was in her favourite chair by the fire. Not that day. She was on her knees at the sofa with her head in her hands. He knew not to disturb her when she was praying, so he walked back to his bungalow.

He washed and shaved and sorted the fire before going back over to Mum's but when he did, he saw that she was still on her knees, hands cupped to her face. At first he thought that it must have been some mighty long prayer that she was praying. She must be saving the souls of the whole country if it was taking her that long, he said to himself. Then instinct told him otherwise. He quickly fumbled the key in the lock and shouted her name, but there was no reply. She was still alive, but she had had a stroke.

Mum lay in hospital for a few days, unable to move. There was just a brief glimmer of recognition when you spoke her name. She would try to open her eyes to show she was still there inside, aware of what was happening around her.

On 1 September 1994, there was a day of celebration across the country. There were fleets of cars in the streets, including the famous Belfast black taxis, all of them honking their horns as they weaved through nationalist areas, and especially along the Falls Road, past the "swalley water" swimming pool of my childhood. Passengers waved their Irish tricolours triumphantly from open car windows. Newspaper headlines shouted the breaking news: the IRA had announced "a complete cessation of military operations".

There was no expression of regret in the IRA ceasefire statement; no indication of remorse for the pain and suffering they had caused countless families during their years of slaughter. Just a grand announcement, which we were all supposed to welcome. We were expected to join them in their supposed "victory celebrations"; we were expected to be thankful they had decided not to kill any of us anymore.

The IRA cessation was to be effective from the first second after midnight on 1 September 1994. My mother decided that would be a good day to die. I held her hand as she lay in her hospital bed, and I told her I loved her. She didn't respond. She didn't need to. I knew she loved me. Maybe her prayers had finally been answered and she found her own peace that day, after years of pain at losing her son and husband. Once more the hospital bedside fan fell silent.

We moved Uncle Geordie into Mum's bungalow after she died. It was warmer than his own, and he loved being there. He would be the last one to die. Now that his sister and brothers had all gone, he didn't enjoy life anymore. Not being able to hear properly or go walking for miles on a clear Belfast morning was not the life he wanted. He no longer followed Cliftonville, or any team, even though by this time, they were regularly winning matches. It was a strange emotion that filled me when I heard that Uncle Geordie had died. I was sad that the man whose name I had been given was gone – yet I was glad he didn't have to spend another silent day, bedridden and depressed. Life "up there", with the Lanky One, the Yank, the Preacher, the Major and his wee sister Etta would be noisy once again . . . Marvellous!

Chapter Eight

Hunting and Shooting

Back in 1977, when I was in my late 20s, my best friend Sam was very much into fishing and hunting, and he would often try to persuade me to join him in his country pursuits. I tried fishing, but the boredom of staring at a river for hours with no result wasn't for me. I concluded that there were enough fish and chip shops throughout Northern Ireland to satisfy my appetite, without having to try to catch the fish myself. Shooting seemed more exciting however, so I applied for a firearms licence, bought the cheapest single-barrelled shotgun I could find, and asked a farmer I knew in Doagh if we could shoot on his land.

Sam's training in the workings of my new shotgun and the art of hunting and shooting seemed all too brief. But, complete with my equally new wellies and waterproofs, I headed off with him around the fields in search of our big game quarry. I doubtless looked the part of gamekeeper or even one of the elite hunting, shooting and fishing set. But that first day of shooting with Sam, which had started off dry and sunny, soon turned wet, cold and miserable, in more ways than one.

I don't know why, but I decided to shoot at some birds flying overhead. They were so high above us that I couldn't identify if they were blackbirds, crows or indeed small, unflustered starlings. In any case, not a single one came close to being hit by my scattered buckshot. Sam wasn't faring much better – so we decided to set up tin cans and try hitting those instead. To tell the truth, I was quickly becoming disillusioned with Sam's marksmanship. His stories of exciting shooting expeditions in previous years seemed less than convincing now, as my new wellies slipped on the grassy banks we were standing on.

Dejected, we finally headed back down the field to the car. Suddenly however Sam stopped, whispered and pointed at the hedge up ahead of us. There was a majestic brown and white hare standing on its back legs, surveying the landscape and our untouched tins. Sam motioned me to slowly lift my gun, which I did. Pressing it against my shoulder, I took aim and fired. The hare jumped slightly in the air and darted left, into the ditch.

Feeling the adrenaline and excitement rising in my legs, I raced to see the results of my perfectly-aimed shot. As we neared the ditch, we could see movement in the brambles, and it was then that I was paralysed by a sound I had never heard before.

The hare was looking directly at me, wide-eyed and bleeding. The squeals of pain and terror didn't belong to any cute, furry animal. They were the screeches of a small, lonely and frightened child, and they pierced the damp air and my conscience like a scalpel through exposed muscle.

It was Sam who put an end to the screams. I walked away, cold and numb, from that once peaceful ditch. I didn't look back. Even now, I don't know why I shot that majestic creature. It was pointless, senseless and unforgivable. The following week, I sold my shotgun back to the gun dealer and returned my licence to the local police station.

Killing wasn't for me.

Chapter Nine

Opening the Parlour Again

You'll have to forgive me if my story doesn't always follow a logical path. It's just the way I remember things now, more than 27 years later. Grief isn't predictable. It writes its own chapters. It takes you down its fragile, twisted staircase of heartache into darkened corners and rooms, where sometimes the doors can slam shut behind you. And the way out starts the journey all over again, but in a different direction.

It had been three weeks since the shooting. The newspapers and television news programmes covered John's murder in daily reports and bulletins during that time. My brother's official police photograph was printed in many of the local papers, plastered across their pages and often accompanied by photographs of me and other family members at his funeral. Some of the articles recounted – incorrectly – how I had been tracked down on my family holiday in Spain by the RUC, with the help of Interpol.

I had read and re-read the dozens of sympathy cards and letters we had been sent, from friends and colleagues, and from people I had never met. Some praised me, saying I had shown great dignity and composure at the funeral. One letter was from a prominent local dignitary who shall remain nameless, offering his heartfelt condolences and saying that I was in his thoughts, after my brother having been blown up in my ice cream parlour. His sympathies were so heartfelt that he hadn't even got the details of the circumstances of John's execution right.

Some of those who wrote expressing their condolences even applauded me for wearing a grey suit instead of the regulation dark one everyone seems to have in their wardrobe for such sombre occasions. They said that such defiance on my part was just right – a way of showing my brother's killers that I was not going to allow them to dictate my emotions. Little did any of them know that my outwardly dignified, composed face was no more than a mask, carefully created to cover how I was feeling inside. And as for the grey suit of celebration and defiance, it was actually the only suit I had at the time that fitted – I've always had trouble losing weight. But as I read them back, such comments on the cards did at least manage to make me smile in the midst of my grief.

During those three weeks, the parlour had stayed closed. I had of course gone back there more than once, to see for myself what had happened that night. There were bunches of flowers resting on the damp pavement beside the door. Kind, sympathetic gestures from unnamed customers and local shopkeepers. I gathered up these bouquets and blooms, and brought them inside to the warmth of the parlour. I then arranged them carefully on one of the tables and set the display at the window for passers-by to see.

Before my first visit, friends had already got the keys of the parlour from me, and gone in to clean away the traces of murder as best they could. However there were still some black smudges here and there on the glass counters and on the meter box on the wall: the tell-tale signs of a crime scene expert searching for the fingerprints of a killer or killers. Dull white patches dotted the pink walls in the places where well-meaning friends had filled in the holes left by the bullets that hadn't hit their intended targets that night – Polyfilla-ed plasters, covering the cracks in a life that had changed forever.

As I hesitantly approached the ice cream counter where John had been shot, I wasn't sure what I would find. My mind conjured up all sorts of senseless images. I envisaged seeing him lying there on the floor, face down on the cold tiles, his blood pooling around him. I imagined I might see the chalked outline of his body, drawn on the floor, like you see at the crime scenes in films and TV dramas.

The ice creams in the cabinet looked drab and dried-out. The once vibrant colours were now dull and lifeless, and a frosty scum had formed across the surfaces of the open tubs. The white floor tiles behind the counter looked spotless and shining, however. My friends had done a good job.

Next I walked round to where my brother had fallen behind the counter. Despite my friends' best efforts, there really was no mistaking what had happened there on that fateful night. The two angry holes in one of the floor tiles were about six inches apart, like dark eyes watching me. This was where the chocolate-loving gunman had fired his final two shots in the darkness, as he leaned over the counter and aimed at John lying on the floor. They'd missed.

I knew I had to open the parlour again. I didn't have the heart for it, but knew I didn't have a choice. The place had only been up-and-running for a few months, and we still had debts with the bank and with suppliers. Of course opening again would also in some way show the bastards they hadn't won. But it wasn't a case of being a hero: the stark reality was economics. Even in the midst of disaster and grief, I simply couldn't afford to just shut it down. So we repainted the pink walls and replaced the splintered skirting boards, threw out the half-empty ice cream tubs that had outlived their sell-by dates, and restocked with even more brightly-coloured flavours.

I had initially planned to dig out the floor tile with the bullet holes gouged into it. But I didn't, after all. Maybe a psychiatrist would be able to make some sense of my actions. I just somehow didn't want all traces of what happened to John to be simply removed; I wanted some sort of daily reminder of what had happened to my brother that night. Illogical, I know, but I felt that somehow the tile with its brutal impact marks from the bullets that failed to hit my brother would act as a tribute to his memory.

The damaged floor tile commemorative plaque for John was also a strangely comforting reminder that the gunman's hate-filled final shots hadn't achieve anything. They weren't necessary and hadn't served any purpose. They were simply confirmation of the blind, misguided hate that the killer had for someone he didn't know and didn't even bother taking the time to find out something about.

We opened again on Saturday, 31 October 1988 – Hallowe'en weekend that year. Before we had originally opened Barnam's, my wife Sadie and I had had a discussion about the different ice creams we could do for celebrations such as Christmas, and Easter and of course the children's favourite, Hallowe'en. Originally we had talked about stocking some weird and scary flavours for that weekend, with more disgusting names to satisfy the kids' appetites for all things ghoulish. Maybe "Raspberry Eyeballs", or "Witch's Warts"? It was amazing what you could do with vanilla ice cream and topping sauce.

But we decided now not do any special flavours for the re-opening. We just didn't want to attract too much attention. We also decided not to involve any staff members that weekend. We felt it wouldn't be fair to ask them to go back in until we had decided it was safe. We also weren't even sure if people would be comfortable visiting the parlour again. We wondered if parents would allow their children back to a place where someone had been murdered and two customers had been shot.

Our apprehension was unfounded, however. People did come back. Even on the first day, there was a steady stream of customers. Everyone who came in said how sorry they were about what had happened. Some applauded us for opening again. Meanwhile other shopkeepers were amazed at our courage. None of them knew how nervous and scared my wife and I were feeling, or how close to tears we were throughout that first day. Our emotions were in turmoil, especially when the children we had got to know so well during the past months came back in, hugged us, and told us how much they had missed us and our ice cream.

That first Saturday night was the worst. It was dark outside and every time the door opened, we looked at each new arrival with dread. We locked up that night and went home exhausted, not from the physical demands of the work, but from the fear and grief that had drained us. The Sunday and Monday were much the same. Nothing eventful, just an increasing number of customers coming in with endless words of encouragement, which proved that we were right to open Barnam's again. We scheduled staff shifts for the rest of that week.

On the fourth night after opening, it was my turn to work in the parlour. My wife had worked during the day that Tuesday, so I took over at 6.00 pm with another member of staff, a young girl called Ailish. Throughout the evening, she kept asking me if I was okay, and I tried to reassure her I was just tired. She did most of the work and dealt with everything with the same great care and attention as she had done prior to the murder.

We were both relieved when closing time came. We were just about to lock up, however, when two customers walked in. One stood at the door at the front of the shop, while the other walked up to the counter, where Ailish and I were putting the cones away.

Ailish looked at me, and I knew she was afraid. I told her to go into the kitchen at the back of the shop, and to clean the dishes and tidy up. We had already cleaned and tidied away all the dirty dishes in the kitchen, so she knew I was telling her to go away to somewhere safe, which she gladly did.

"Two sliders, mate," the man at the counter said, as he smiled at me.

"Sorry, we don't sell sliders," I replied, feeling as if I was in a re-run of a drama of which I already knew the ending.

"Aw, yeah that's right, yiz don't sell sliders, just cones." He smirked even more broadly. "I'll have two cones then, two chocolate ones, mate."

His words were deliberate and menacing. I had heard and seen those words before. I had already read them in a statement just a week earlier, when the police had asked me to look at some mugshots and allowed me to read statements from the member of staff who was on duty that night with John, as well as from the two teenage customers.

I glanced at the man standing at the door, and back to the smiler at the counter. I scooped the ice cream into two cones and handed them to him. These guys were deliberately recreating exactly what had happened the night John was murdered. I didn't know whether to run or scream or faint. The one at the counter handed me his coins, the exact amount needed to pay for the two cones. He then walked towards the door, turned back and cheerily quipped, "Nice chocolate, mate," as he handed one of the cones to his friend. They went out of the parlour together, laughing.

I locked the door and watched them get into a small red van parked about 30 feet away. I switched off some of our lights and Ailish came out of the kitchen, shaking. I didn't know what to do. Should I telephone the police, and have them come racing to the parlour to arrest the guys in the red van? For what – asking for sliders? Buying chocolate cones? I'd cause a scene at the parlour and put the final nail in the coffin of business.

I too was shaking, with a mixture of fear and anger. I was seething inside. But I didn't want Ailish to panic anymore, so I told her everything would be okay. I suggested we get our coats and the money from the till and go straight out to my car. It was parked directly outside, just a few feet away. She asked me if the guys had gone. I told her that no, they were still sitting in the red van further along the road, eating their cones. She was scared. So was I – but I had to do this. As I walked out to the car, unlocked it and called Ailish out to join me, the two guys threw their unfinished cones out of the van's open windows. I went back into the parlour, set the alarm and quickly locked up, before getting into my car and driving off.

The van moved off as well. It was about three car lengths behind us, but I could clearly see it in my rearview mirror, even in the darkness. As I drove down the Lisburn Road, heading for where Ailish lived, I decided that I couldn't risk dropping her off at her house and thereby letting the guys in the van know where she lived.

I turned right, off the Lisburn Road and in the direction of Malone Road. The guys in the van did the same. I turned left on Malone Road. They did the same. I turned left again, back towards the Lisburn Road. They did the same. There was no mistaking it: they were following us. Ailish started to cry.

I decided that these bastards were deliberately trying to scare us. Whoever they were, they had to be connected in some way to those who had killed

John – they clearly knew about the sliders and the chocolate flavour. But if they wanted to kill me, I reasoned, they could have done it in the parlour. So most likely, they were just trying to frighten us. And they were succeeding.

The more upset Ailish got, the angrier I became – I was madder than I had been for a long time. I noted the van's registration number. And I decided, "F**k them! If they want to play games, then f**k them!" I speeded up. Ailish looked at me with renewed fear in her eyes. "Don't worry," I said, as calmly as I could, as I drove past her house. I assured her I would get her home safely. Then I speeded up some more. The bastards were still close behind.

I headed for Great Victoria Street and College Square. I deliberately stayed on the left, giving the impression I was intending to travel straight on through College Avenue and past the Technical College. They were very close behind us now. At the last minute, I swerved right into Wellington Place. The guys in the van hadn't time to react, and had to travel straight on. Had they also swerved right at that point, they probably would have ended up crashing into the statue of Reverend Dr Henry Cooke, the "Black Man", which stands on a high plinth outside Royal Belfast Academical Institution.

Racing down Wellington Place past the City Hall, I kept looking in my rearview mirror, expecting the lights of the van to appear out of the darkness at any moment. But there was nothing. They hadn't turned back to continue the pursuit. It seemed that they had achieved what they set out to do that night. They hadn't planned to kill the ice cream man's brother this time – just to scare the bejasus out of him and one of his female staff.

I kept up my speed as I travelled round the City Hall and back towards the Lisburn Road, all the while hoping to be stopped for speeding by some police in the area. None were about. I dropped Ailish off at her house. She had calmed down, but was now worried about me getting home safely. I told her I was going to Donegall Pass Police Station close by before heading home.

I went in to the station and asked for the detectives I knew were handling my brother's murder investigation there. Thankfully one of them, Bob, was on duty that night. I took him through the details: how the guys had asked me for sliders and chocolate ice cream, and how they obviously knew what the gunman had said to John on the night of the murder. I also gave him the registration number of the red van and a description of the two guys.

Bob went away and checked the registration of the van. He didn't give me any names, but told me it belonged to a guy with known PIRA connections. He reassured me by saying, "George, if these guys wanted you dead, they would have done it. I think they hate the fact that you have opened the parlour again – and you are a policeman's brother, so they probably want to scare you into closing again. I can't obviously tell you what to do, but don't let these bastards win."

Easy for Bob to say. He didn't have to go back the next night and every night after that. But I was determined that they wouldn't win. I didn't care anymore. We had worked hard to make Barnam's a place of fun for families and especially children in Belfast, at a time when it was a place of sectarian hatred. I would be going back the next night, and every night. Bob told me he would try to get covert photos of the guys he thought might be involved, to see if I would recognise them as the two who had harassed us that night.

By the time I got home, Ailish had already telephoned my house and told my wife what had happened and asked if I was okay. When Sadie said I hadn't come home yet, both she and Ailish became concerned. Thankfully, I arrived home just before Sadie was about to start phoning friends and family in an unnecessary panic.

I rang back Ailish and told her what I had done at the police station, asking her not to tell any other staff members what had happened. A terrible thing to do, but I had to decide what was best and what my next move would be. The next day I told Ailish she didn't have to work at Barnam's anymore. However, she surprised me by saying that she wasn't going to let them dictate what she did with her life either, and that she would be back in Barnam's as usual for her next scheduled shift a few days later. A brave young girl, whose courage made me even more determined.

The next day Sadie and I went back to Barnam's to work alongside the scheduled staff. We didn't need so many of us to be there, but we had to get through this and I felt I had to be there to support them and sort out whatever was going to happen next. So we found ourselves in a crazy situation, created by simple financial necessity and reinforced by bloody-minded determination.

Bob suggested having plain clothes detectives watch Barnam's in the following weeks. On numerous occasions during that time, I telephoned Donegall Pass station to report suspicious vehicles, only to be told that they were covert police or army vehicles, tasked with watching me and Barnam's.

Some of the police officers sent to covertly keep an eye on me would actually come into the parlour to buy ice cream and chat about the investigation into the killing! They were incredibly frank in how they spoke about it. Some gave me the names of the key suspects, thereby raising my hopes in days before I discovered how poor the RUC was at gathering evidence. As I would find out all too quickly, they were good at knowing what was going on and who was doing what, and sometimes they were even good at stopping the culprits – but they were not good at catching them and putting them away.

I told Bob that the covert surveillance operatives were not very professional, if I could identify them so easily, and I suggested that they should simply stop their rather laughable efforts. And apparently they did, for I didn't notice them hanging around anymore after that. Although maybe they just got better at their jobs!

In any case Bob visited me in Barnam's the following week to show me photographs they had covertly taken of some possible suspects. I was able to identify the two smirking customers who had followed us in the red van. Bob assured me that the police would continue to watch them, and again suggested that he felt they simply wanted to intimidate us into closing the shop again.

I never saw the two men again. In the following months, however, there were regular incidents of intimidation. Mostly in the form of "subtle" remarks from male customers, directed at me when I was working shifts in Barnam's. There were also regular nuisance telephone calls, some silent and others deliberately threatening. I endured this persistent intimidation throughout most of the early part of 1989. But it was affecting me and I was drained, although I didn't share this with anyone, not even my wife.

By June 1989, things had spiralled out of control. I was at the end of my tether and, in hindsight, probably heading for a nervous breakdown. My small publishing company had closed down, and my dad's health was deteriorating rapidly. One night that month, as I was preparing to lock up the parlour, the phone rang and I answered, thinking it was my wife. A male voice told me to listen very carefully. Speaking calmly and directly, he told me to remove the money from the cash register. He then instructed me to put the cash in the money bag and place it in a black plastic bin bag, along with any rubbish from the shop. He said that I should then leave the shop, lock up and place the black plastic bin bag on the pavement outside.

He warned me not to try and be clever, and told me to drive home to Bangor without stopping anywhere. He told me not to make any telephone calls after he had hung up, and that I shouldn't try phoning the police; nor should I stop at the police station on my way down the Lisburn Road. He assured me I was being watched.

Call it stupid or cowardly, but I did what he said. Looking back now, I know I was so mentally and physically empty by this time that I had simply given up. I dumped the black plastic rubbish bag containing that day's takings on the pavement, and drove home. At the time I told no one. Not my wife, not the staff, not the police.

I have no idea who made the call that night. I don't know who picked up the rubbish bag after I left. It could have been Republicans, or Loyalists, or even local criminals who sensed my vulnerability. It didn't matter to me who it was.

I sold Barnam's one week later, paid off its debts and never went back. Neither I nor any of my family have any connection to any retail outlet still trading under the Barnam's name.

Chapter Ten

The Gibraltar Three: March 1988

My brother John's murder by members of the West Belfast Brigade of the Provisional IRA had its roots in events which took place seven months earlier and almost 1,300 miles away from Belfast, in Gibraltar. This was something which was confirmed to me by some of John's colleagues in the weeks after his death, when, unsolicited by me, they shared with me the conclusions of their intelligence-gathering efforts.

On Sunday, 6 March 1988, three members of an active service unit of the Provisional IRA were in Gibraltar. It has been suggested that they were there to launch a bombing operation against the British Crown Forces stationed on the Rock. It has been surmised that their intended target was the band and guard of the First Battalion of the Royal Anglian Regiment, who were to take part in that week's changing-of-the-guard ceremony outside the Governor's official residence on Tuesday, 8 March.

Those IRA members were Mairéad Farrell, Daniel McCann and Sean Savage. Whether it was down to expert covert surveillance efforts or, as seems more likely, the result of specific intelligence provided to them by a high-ranking informer within the IRA, British security forces were already aware of the IRA team's intentions. Accordingly, the SAS was waiting to ambush and thwart the terrorists in their planned attack.

Fearing – incorrectly, as it later transpired – that the three experienced IRA members were armed, had already planted the car bomb and were ready to detonate it at any moment, the SAS personnel were in a heightened state of readiness.

At approximately 3.40 pm on that sunny afternoon, Mairéad Farrell and Daniel McCann were shot dead as they casually walked past the Shell garage on Winston Churchill Avenue, the busy main road that leads to the airport and the frontier crossing with Spain. There are conflicting reports about how many shots were fired by the SAS marksmen, however Mairéad Farrell was shot at least five or six times, while Dan McCann sustained around eight bullet wounds. Both died instantly in this merciless hail of gunfire. Sean Savage, who was following close behind, was hit by at least 16 bullets as he tried to make his escape along Smith Dorrien Avenue. He too would die at the scene.

In a follow-up debriefing, the security forces indicated that they considered that Dan McCann, in making an aggressive gesture towards the bag he was carrying, was about to detonate a bomb with some sort of remote control device. They said they had shot him instantly, in order to prevent him doing this. It was confirmed in the same statement that Mairéad Farrell had been seen to make a similarly suspicious move towards her handbag, which was the reason she too had been shot instantly. The SAS members in question also stated that they had seen Sean Savage move his hand within his pocket and that, fearing he was about to explode the bomb, they had shot him multiple times to render him incapable of carrying out this act.

It was later acknowledged that all three IRA operatives were unarmed at the time they were shot, and that none of them was carrying any remote control device. In follow-up investigations, it was also admitted that, although materials for a car bomb were found two days later in a car in Spain that had been used by the IRA team, the car identified as belonging to them during their time in Gibraltar did not contain a bomb.

From that day onwards, the three IRA volunteers became known as "the Gibraltar Three".

British Prime Minister at the time, Margaret Thatcher stated that the operation by the SAS had been a blow to the IRA. However, even as the bodies of the Gibraltar Three were being returned to Belfast for burial, accompanied by Belfast Sinn Féin councillor, Joe Austin, it would appear that some members of the West Belfast Brigade of the Provisional IRA were making plans to wreak revenge for the killing of their comrades in Gibraltar.

Seven months later, my brother John, an off-duty RUC officer with no connection to the killing of Mairéad Farrell, Daniel McCann and Sean Savage, ended up dead. Apparently, as grotesque as it might sound, he was simply murdered by members of that West Belfast IRA Brigade, in retaliation for the killing of the Gibraltar Three – and as a sort of honour-killing tribute to their fallen comrades and friends.

Chapter Eleven

Milltown Cemetery

On 16 March 1988, ten days after the Gibraltar killings, an ambush in Belfast's Milltown Cemetery was witnessed by millions of people worldwide, who were able to watch live as the dramatic and terrifying events unfolded on their television screens.

Thousands of mourners, including Sinn Féin leaders, Gerry Adams and Martin McGuinness, were attending the funerals of the Gibraltar Three at the Republican plot in the cemetery. News-hungry journalists and camera crews from across the world had also descended upon Milltown to capture the images of the historic funerals.

As the coffins were lowered into the freshly dug earth, a series of explosions shattered the graveyard silence. Initially confused, then suddenly realising they were under attack, the mourners tried to take cover behind the surrounding headstones.

A man with long hair and a moustache, wearing a bulky anorak, gloves and a cap, was firing a Browning 9 mm handgun and hurling hand grenades towards the open graves, as television crews kept their cameras rolling. For many mourners, particularly women and children, the perceived protection of the gravestones proved completely inadequate. Over 60 received shrapnel injuries, as the explosions tore shards of marble and granite from the headstones, which ripped and slashed into those attempting to take shelter.

Continuing to fire, the gunman retreated and then started jogging towards the M1 motorway, several hundred yards away. It was at this stage that hundreds of men, themselves unarmed and apparently thinking nothing of their own safety, ran after him, down through the cemetery. As they did so, the gunman periodically stopped and turned to face them. In an attempt to halt or slow their advance, he randomly fired at the swarming mass now in pursuit, throwing a number of additional grenades in their direction before resuming his proposed break for freedom. By this time, he had run out of ammunition for the Browning, so he tossed it away and, taking his back-up

Ruger pistol from his anorak, continued to fire at the advancing crowd. Mud-filled explosions erupted from the grassy no-man's-land between him and his pursuers, as each hastily thrown grenade fell short of its intended target. The gunman's cap fell from his head onto the marshy land, as he neared the end of his planned dash to the motorway. A white van could be seen, speeding away just below the graveyard before he got there.

The crowd eventually caught the fugitive on the motorway, by which time he had exhausted his supply of ammunition and grenades. His escape plan, if he had one, was falling apart. He was beaten unconscious by some of his pursuers, and was just being bundled into a car when the police arrived. Had the crowd managed to complete their abduction of the gunman, it is likely he would have been taken to IRA members in West Belfast, who would have been keen to interrogate him to establish his identity. Once they had done so, it is likely that they would have killed this previously unknown Loyalist gunman, Michael Stone, in retaliation for his unprecedented one-man attack on the funerals of the Gibraltar Three.

By the end of that day, three more names had been added to Northern Ireland's catalogue of Troubles deaths. These were Caoimhin MacBradaigh (Kevin Brady), an IRA member, and Thomas McErlean and John Murray, two civilian mourners.

One of the guns Michael Stone used during the Milltown attack was a Speed Six Ruger .357 Magnum revolver. The serial numbers on this gun had been expertly removed. Members of the crowd who caught Michael Stone on the motorway that day managed to retrieve the Ruger, and it would end up in the hands of the West Belfast Brigade of the IRA. A photograph of the Ruger, along with other items retrieved from Michael Stone that day in the cemetery, was published in *An Phoblacht* the following week.

Chapter Twelve

Left-Footers

During the dark days of the Troubles in the 1970s and 1980s, I worked in advertising, mostly with the *Belfast Telegraph*. I was used to being involved in the organisation and marketing of all types of events. This could entail anything from planning the annual in-house staff training seminar to the handling of weekly advertisements for small and bigger shops throughout Belfast – such as the Co-op in York Street or Crazy Prices with their "pile-'em-high – sell-'em-cheap" mantra for tempting customers in.

That was the bottom line at the time for too many battle-scarred local traders, struggling to stay in business: getting customers through their doors instead of those of their competitors – that was the only goal in town. The bank manager was always looming in the background. The tills had to be kept ringing, in tune with the sirens of fire engines as they raced to the latest bomb explosion.

Some shops were glad they even had doors to close at the end of every day. And many members of many families said a silent prayer, when their dad or their mum or brother or sister came home safe and well after locking those doors. Some didn't make it home to safety; some were executed on the doorstep they thought was a refuge.

One of the most satisfying and genuinely uplifting marketing initiatives I was privileged to be involved with was the brainchild of a man who is sadly no longer with us. He was Stanley Reid, who owned Reid's Shoes in Sandy Row. Like so many others, Stanley no doubt had his own bank manager reminding him of the balance on his statements. But he cared more about people than he did about commercial profit. And just like every other business in the city, Stanley did his best to come up with successful advertisements that would bring customers to his shop, and he somehow managed to keep the doors open and his loyal staff paid during those very difficult times.

One day in 1976, I called with him to discuss a Stock Clearance advertisement he wanted to put in the *Belfast Telegraph*. Stanley said he had been thinking long and hard about an idea he had come up with. He didn't want it to sound like a clever gimmick, and it was something he genuinely wanted to do, despite the cost.

He had, he explained, read too many stories in the newspapers about people who had been maimed and injured in the bombings and shootings that were so prevalent in those dark days. He had been particularly upset after reading about yet another person losing a leg in a bomb blast, and he said that he wanted to place a simple advertisement in the newspaper, saying that anyone who had lost a leg could come and buy any pair of shoes at his shop, but that they would only have to pay for the shoe they needed.

It wasn't devised as a clever marketing idea; it wasn't aimed at getting him lots of publicity; it wasn't a money-making concept. It was simply the heart-warming idea of a man who considered himself lucky in life and who wanted to extend a hand of true friendship and concern to people, whose lives had been dealt such a cruel and crippling blow.

When I grew up on the Shankill Road, I would often hear my fellow Protestants referring to Roman Catholics as "left-footers". I don't know where the expression originated from, but there was a strange local Belfast saying along these lines: "Oh, yer man's a Catholic. He kicks with his left foot." Some people say it alludes to the belief that in days gone by, Catholic farm workers used their left foot to push the spade into the ground when digging turf, while Protestants used their right foot. How true such a bizarre statement might be, I will leave you to decide, according to your own imagination and beliefs!

The week after that advertisement appeared, Stanley recounted how one man who had come into his shop had made him laugh. I laughed too when Stanley told me the full story. The man in question had said that he was a "left-footer", but that he was now a "right-footer", since he needed to buy one shoe for his right foot, having lost the left one in a bomb explosion somewhere between Royal Avenue and the City Hall. That man's typical Belfast black humour that day taught us all something.

Stanley sold a lot of shoes the week after the advert appeared, although he probably didn't make much extra money, as he was selling individual shoes at half the price of a pair. But he gained more riches than money could ever buy – he helped a lot of "left-footers" and "right-footers" to feel that someone cared about what they had suffered, regardless of which foot they kicked with.

Chapter Thirteen

Dunkirk: 1940

They were two young lads in their early 20s, always willing to take risks in search of adventure. Two fresh-faced scallywags in a vast sea of faces, tossed together and out of their depth, in every sense this time. Holding onto each other in the lashing waves. Holding onto life. All around them, the chaos of an army in retreat. The sounds of war were in their ears and the cold of the sea was in their bones.

Youthful dreams of the adventure of war were now a harsh, brutal reality, as the two willed each other to stay alive. They could see the fishing boats coming. Tiny, bobbing rescue specks on the horizon brought a sense of hope tinged with fear to these two young soldiers, who found themselves on the beach at Dunkirk in Northern France on 30 May 1940.

They were just two among the hundreds of thousands in the water that day: spread out, wading shoulder-deep for hours – a human oil slick across the surface of the sea. Some were old; many were far too young. All were far from home, countless miles from the comfort of terraced houses in streets across England, Scotland, Wales and Ireland, north and south. In the darkening hours, as they swayed with the water that sucked at their thoughts, most were no doubt remembering loved ones back home: their mothers, girlfriends, wives; their smiling children. Perhaps they heard Vera Lynn's voice in their heads, singing the words of her famous song: "We'll meet again/Don't know where/Don't know when …"

These comforting memories of home, undiluted by the distance between them, warmed the frightened and weakening men from within, helping to give them the strength to stay alive. Sadly however, many would only have those last memories, and they never would meet their loved ones back home again. Not in this life anyway.

The sea threw those two young lads together that day in 1940. It chose them well. One was my dad, Private John Larmour, a Protestant from the Shankill Road area of Belfast; the other was Sergeant John McCann, a Catholic from

This photograph of John was taken on holiday in Portugal just a few weeks before he was murdered in Barnam's on 11 October 1988.

All dressed up in our best outfits for the family album. I am on the left aged about five, with my big brother John and our sister Jean.

A reassuring arm from my big brother, as we sit in the sunshine on the windowsill outside our house in Northumberland Street.

Happy school days at Charter's Memorial School *(above, I am seated first left)* and Argyle Primary School *(below, I am second left standing)*.

Our favourite after-school activity was playing Cowboys and Indians up the road in Woodvale Park – slapping our thighs to make our imaginary horses gallop faster across the prairie.

I am second from right, squashed between cousins Bill, Patricia and Bob, on the big windowsill outside our house in Northumberland Street. Cousin John McA is on the left, kneeling on the ground beside my brother John, who is smiling and posing for the camera.

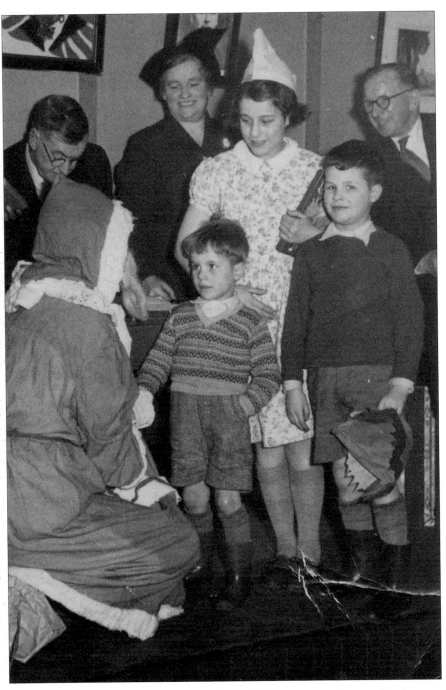

I seem mesmerised by Santa (Uncle Hughie) while John, as usual, poses for the camera and sister Jean tries to tell her wee brothers what to do.

Santa (Uncle Hughie) has his arm around sister Jean and a hand on my shoulder, while John clutches his new children's annual, and cousins Patricia, John McA, Roberta and twins Bill and Bob pose for the camera.

My brother John was always the handsome and sporty one in the family. A goal-scoring genius on the football pitch for many local teams and not bad on the golf course but I doubt he would have made it to Centre Court Wimbledon.

John looking very happy, fit and healthy in his thirties *(above)* and as a very serious six year old *(right)*.

My Dad's Burma Star Medal

My Dad joined the Army (Royal Artillery) at the outbreak of World War Two. He served in Europe and was evacuated at Dunkirk. This picture of him was drawn by a homeless man in India before Dad travelled on to fight in Burma.

Mum and Dad got married before he headed off to an uncertain future in the battlefields of Europe and the jungles of Burma in World War Two.

The reality of war soon dawned on my Dad when, in his early twenties, he found himself on the beach at Dunkirk along with hundreds of thousands of other soldiers fighting for their lives. As he and other soldiers swam out to meet the little rescue boats that were heading to Dunkirk he found himself exhausted in the waves and on the brink of death in that cold, heartless sea of defeat. Out of the thousands of men in the sea that day he found one particular soldier who was also from his native Belfast. Sergeant John McCann and my Dad clung to each other, saving each other from drowning, until they were thankfully picked up by one of the small fishing boats.

Off Dunkirk the Channel Was Like Henley on a Regatta Day

Cross-Channel steamers are notoriously small and responsive to the swell of the Straits of Dover. But thousands of men crossed from Dunkirk in small open boats and some, as in the photograph above, were even towed across in strings of rowing boats.

This view of an escorting destroyer at full speed (above) was taken from the deck of a trawler by a member of the crew. The trawler was one of many packed with Allied troops from Dunkirk.
Photos, "Daily Mirror," Planet News, Associated Press, "The Times"

...y were the small craft (above) of the mixed "ferry ...rting French destroyers (top right) was occupied by A... Navy, the Royal Navy and the captains of the...

My Dad's
Dunkirk Medal

Right: Dad holding my sister Jean during a welcome trip home from fighting in Europe during World War Two.

He was sent to fight in Burma and didn't see his baby daughter again for another three years.

(Courtesy McCann family)

John McCann (above) with his wife Sally and my Mum and Dad (right) enjoying old age.

My dad, a Protestant from the Shankill Road and John McCann, a Catholic from the Andersonstown Road in Belfast, saved each other from drowning in the sea at Dunkirk in 1940.

These two young lads didn't care about religion or sectarian bigotry, they just wanted to go back home to their families in Belfast. They remained friends for the rest of their lives.

Mum and Dad in happier times at my wedding to Sadie in April 1971. Little did they know that the future would bring unbearable heartache for all our family.

John was 'Best Man' at my wedding and had not joined the RUC at that stage, hence the 1970s hairstyle complete with sideburns.

MR JIMMY HASTY – MURDERED 11 OCTOBER 1974

Mr Jimmy Hasty receiving the award of 'Player of the Year' in 1963 at Dundalk FC. That year he helped them become the first Irish team to win a European match when they beat FC Zurich 2-1 in a thrilling away game.

A smiling Paul on his daddy's shoulders.   Mr Hasty with baby Paul and son Martin.

Jimmy Hasty lost his left arm in an accident on his first day at work, aged just 14. Despite his disability he went on to become a very skilled football player and played professionally in the 1960s for various local clubs in Northern Ireland and was a top goal scorer for League of Ireland team, Dundalk FC.

I held Mr Hasty as he died on the pavement in Brougham Street, Belfast on 11 October 1974, when he was shot a number of times on his way to work by a Loyalist gunman, apparently for simply being a Catholic. Fourteen years later, in 1988 on that same date (11 October), my brother John was murdered by the IRA for simply being a Protestant and a member of the RUC. Mr Hasty's young wife Margaret was left to bring up their two young sons Martin, seven, and Paul, aged just two.

(Photographs courtesy Hasty family)

the Andersonstown area of the same city. They were two young men, who didn't care about religion or politics – they just wanted to live and be able to go home to their families back in Belfast. And they would never forget that they owed their lives to each other and, when they managed to meet up again after the war, they wouldn't allow petty sectarian bigotry to spoil something so important.

Those two men, even as they grew older and lived through the years of bitterness and division that ripped our society apart, never allowed anything to weaken their bond or tarnish their shared experiences. They continued to meet regularly in Belfast, and to remember and understand the true meaning of friendship. Whenever they met, these two men would hug each other as brothers. They remained friends until they died.

Sadly, our society continues to label people because of their religion or where they were born, keeping us divided. I'm glad my dad and John McCann showed it doesn't have to be like that; they showed by example that there is a better way.

When my dad was finally rescued that day in Dunkirk by one of the little ships that came from across the channel, he had already removed all his wet clothes to stop himself from sinking and drowning. His rescuers placed a blanket over him in the boat to keep him warm. He brought that blanket home with him, and my mum kept it to remind her of the day he was saved at Dunkirk. Now, 75 years after that fateful day, I hold that old blanket with its frayed tassels, and it reminds me of two young Belfast scallywags who chose friendship over sectarian bigotry.

Chapter Fourteen

The Envelope

There are always moments when you suddenly realise that someone is dead. I don't mean when you get the dreaded phone call, or when you're otherwise first told that someone has died. Nor the moment when you see them dead, or when you're at their funeral. I mean when a death becomes truly real for you, in one of those specific moments in your day-to-day life when it just hits you.

It happens usually when you least expect it. These little unforeseen moments most often just sneak up on you and catch you, unguarded, during periods of ordinary life. And they're different for every person, of course. It's in these moments you realise that a person who meant so much to you, who was such a part of your everyday life, isn't part of it anymore – and never will be again. They're never coming back. You can't meet them for a drink after work or a quick coffee during the day. You can't chat on the phone or call in, unannounced, to ask their advice. You can't ever again watch them smile or touch them, hold them or smell their perfume or aftershave.

I remember this happening to me when my Granny died – my mum's mother. She was called Margaret, but everyone called her "Mazie". I was 20 years old when Granny had been taken into hospital, suffering from pneumonia. People had joked that we would have to "put her down", as she would never die of her own accord. She had suffered seven heart attacks in her life and survived them all. She lived until she was 92, by which time she had had enough and wanted to die.

I remember sitting with Granny at her bedside at home, reminiscing together. She wasn't in any pain – but she said she was simply tired, and wanted to go now. Then she looked at me and asked me to put the pillow over her face, to help her on her way.

I told her that I wouldn't be able to live with myself if I did that, and that I knew she wouldn't want me to have that on my conscience. "I suppose God doesn't want me, then," she said, and then she just held my hand.

Granny eventually couldn't be kept at home any longer and had to be taken into hospital, where she died alone a few days later. I hated that. Afterwards, I swore I would never let that happen to one of my family again; that I would always be there for them in those final moments.

Months after her death, I was searching for something when I came across Granny's big brown purse. She had had it for years – it had seemed to last forever! Mum had obviously kept it as a reminder of her mother and intended that it would last for more years in her care. And that was the moment it hit me; the moment Granny's death became real. A seemingly small, insignificant moment – and yet the memory hit me, and I knew that she was never going to be in my life again.

I then remembered how, when I was about seven, I had stolen two big old pennies from Granny's purse and spent the money on sweets. I didn't need to steal that money – she would have given me every penny she had, if I had asked. But as a seven-year-old, stealing those two pennies was something exciting for me. And I never did get caught. As I looked at Granny's purse that day, months after she had died and remembered stealing from her, I took some coins from my pocket and placed them inside. "Sorry, Granny," I whispered, as I put her purse back in the drawer. I hope she heard me.

On another occasion, I witnessed someone else, a stranger, experience one of these moments too. It happened one day when I was driving up the M2 motorway. My own dad was no longer alive at that time. Suddenly I saw a woman, standing beside her car on the hard shoulder, looking bewildered. I'm sure initially I gave her the kind of disdainful look that all male drivers save for such occasions, when they see a woman driver on the side of the road, looking at a flat tyre on her car, apparently hoping that it might fix itself if she stares long enough at it.

However I stopped anyway, and pulled in just ahead of her on the hard shoulder. As I got out of my car and walked back towards her, I could see that she was crying and kicking the tyre.

"Ach for God's sake, love, don't be worryin' yourself. I'll have it fixed in no time. No bother. C'mon now. Calm yourself. It's only a puncture – give us your keys and I'll get your spare out of the boot."

She just stared at me and cried even more. "I got a puncture two weeks ago and I changed it. I can change a wheel – I'm not f**kin' stupid, you know!"

"Wow, I never said you were stupid, love. But let me guess. You didn't get the puncture fixed, did you? So you've no spare now. I'm right, aren't I?"

"Yes, you're right! My dad told me to make sure I got it fixed, but –" The tears started again. "Well … I forgot."

"There you go. See, you should always listen to your dad. Dads always know best, so they do."

Then she just blurted out that her daddy had died the previous week – and I realised that she had just had one of those moments when his death had become real for her. As she stood on that hard shoulder, staring at the flat tyre and weeping, she had suddenly realised that he would never be a part of her life again.

So I took her and her spare wheel to the nearest garage, where we got it fixed and we returned to her car, and replaced the flat wheel with the new one. She gave me a hug; her tears had finally stopped. I'm glad she had someone she could share that moment of realisation with; someone who understood its importance.

After John's murder, I was alone when one of those moments of awareness hit me. It didn't come with the shock of touching his cheek that day when he lay cold in his coffin. It was sparked by something else, something equally painful, a few weeks after he was killed.

The envelope in my hand looked like the kind that hard-working, grime-stained factory workers were handed every Friday back in the 1950s and 1960s. People were paid in cash in those days, before there were fancy bank accounts or direct cash transfers. Instead, each worker would be given an odd-shaped little brown envelope, with some official printed text on the front, along with the worker's name, written in blue ink. Inside they would find a slip of paper, detailing the hours they had toiled that week, and a bundle of neatly folded notes which they would count out straight away, to make sure they had been given the wages they were due. It was as if their life that week was summed up in that small, sealed brown envelope.

But the envelope I had in my hands now was different. It had been delivered from the Belfast City Hospital, and on the front was the printed heading: "Patient's Personal Possessions", as well as, in scrawled blue ink and barely legible, the name "John Larmour – Male" and, itemised at the bottom: "Digital Watch (1), Gold Ring (1)".

It had probably been written in haste by some overworked nurse who had been given the job of cataloguing these final mementoes. My brother's life, summed up in a sealed brown envelope; his final reward, like some parting pay slip, for doing a job others wouldn't have dreamed of doing.

The package was too small of course to contain his clothes – they had already been discarded. In fact they had been cut off him that fateful night, as the paramedics and hospital staff fought in vain to stem the flow of lifeblood that seeped away from his body.

There was no immaculately pressed uniform with its shiny buttons; no black shoes polished to perfection. He wasn't in his police uniform that night. But that didn't matter to his killers. He was still the enemy, and less of a threat, dressed in his neat casual slacks and bright polo shirt. The trademark camouflage of an off-duty policeman, trying to blend in. More suitable for a golf outing.

It was early morning. I wasn't fully awake. Since I had received the envelope, I kept looking at it, wondering what to do with it. Now at last I quickly tore open the flap and tipped the contents into my palm. At this, the pre-set alarm on John's watch suddenly went off. Five or six harsh screeches that startled me. I didn't know how to switch the alarm off, but it didn't matter – slowly the screeches got softer and weaker, until they finally died and the watch lay silent in my hand, along with John's ring.

At first I didn't realise what I was seeing as I looked at my fingers. The brownish colour initially confused me. It wasn't like in the movies, when John Wayne fought the Apaches – vivid and ruby red. My brother's watch and ring were covered in the same dirty, brown, dried substance that I had seen on my father's photo of the little Japanese boy. Blood. Was the nurse too busy that night to clean the smears of murder from my brother's few belongings, before placing them in the envelope?

That's the moment it hit me: my brother was dead and he would never be a part of my life again. The cold reality of his death was there, inescapable, in my hands. As I tried to wash away the painful memories and the blood of my dead brother from the ring and watch, the tears wouldn't stop flowing. I wept with a force that scared me. I was distraught, but I was also angry. I wanted to grab that nurse and shake her and scream at her, for subjecting me to this additional haunting reminder. Another one of those moments of realisation from which there is no escape.

I cleaned the ring and gave it to John's son, Gavin, who was barely 13 at the time. It was of course too big for his small fingers then, but one day it would fit okay. One day he could wear it and hopefully it would help him remember some of the good moments of his short time with his dad.

I kept the watch but never wore it. It felt heavy on my wrist. It lay in my bedside drawer. It always made sure I knew it was there – the alarm sounded every morning at the same time. A typical gesture from my brother, making sure I didn't forget him. That alarm managed to maintain its wake-up call for over a year. The battery eventually lost its power: the watch has stayed silent ever since.

Chapter Fifteen

Waterstones Bookshop: 1999

I didn't select him from one of the shelves; didn't go searching under "L" in the row upon row of author's names. I didn't pick him up and speed-read through some of the pages to savour the words he had written. I didn't need to do any of this: he was right there in front of me. The man himself, that is, not one of his many books. I don't know why I was so surprised. Where else, other than a bookshop, would you expect to find one of Ireland's greatest poets?

My hesitation was caused by a degree of uncertainty. It was him alright – of that I had no doubt. Even with his back turned to me, I knew it was him. I had seen his photograph and his face, many times throughout the previous few years, in magazines and newspapers and on television. The big broad frame, the long coat and a partial glimpse of his pure white beard. There was no mistaking him.

I didn't know what to do. I had always looked on Waterstones bookshop in downtown Belfast as just a step down from the local library, in terms of the respect which should be observed when browsing through its shelves. It was a place of contemplative silence, where you knew not to disturb other book lovers engrossed in their prospective literary selections.

Should I just walk on past and not acknowledge him? It was 1999, and almost eleven years since my brother John's murder. This man had never met me, so why would I speak to him? Why should he want to speak to me? Why interrupt his studious search for whatever new book he was looking for?

Soon the decision was made for me. As if sensing my presence, he turned and looked straight at me. So I said in an embarrassed whisper, "Hello, Mr Longley – I'm the Ice Cream Man's brother."

I remember the first time I read the poem, "The Ice-Cream Man". My mum had heard Michael Longley reading it on the radio, and she had asked my sister to search for whichever of his books would have the poem in it. One day when I was visiting her, Mum simply handed me the book, asking

if I had read the poem. I hadn't. So I flicked through the pages, found it and
started to read.

THE ICE-CREAM MAN

> Rum and raisin, vanilla, butter-scotch, walnut, peach:
> You would rhyme off the flavours. That was before
> They murdered the ice-cream man on the Lisburn Road
> And you bought carnations to lay outside his shop.
> I named for you all the wild flowers of the Burren
> I had seen in one day: thyme, valerian, loosestrife,
> Meadowsweet, tway blade, crowfoot, ling, angelica,
> Herb robert, marjoram, cow parsley, sundew, vetch,
> Mountain avens, wood sage, ragged robin, stitchwort,
> Yarrow, lady's bedstraw, bindweed, bog pimpernel.

I'm not a great lover of poetry, and at first I didn't know what to think of
the poem as I skimmed through it quickly. It seemed just a ridiculously short
piece of poetry, which mentioned the ice cream man being murdered on the
Lisburn Road, followed by simple lists of ice cream flavours and wildflower
names. But as I re-read it a number of times that day, I was somehow taken
on a peaceful and emotional journey, and found tears welling in my eyes. I
started to understand the beautiful simplicity of Michael Longley's words,
and the many hidden layers that slowly emerged. This was a master excelling
at his craft.

The poem was written to his young daughter, Sarah, who, like dozens of
other children in the area, regularly bought ice cream from us. And just like
those other wide-eyed children, every time she came into the parlour, she
would look at all the flavours and rhyme off all their names, before finally
choosing one to spend her pocket money on that week. This was a ritual that
we quickly came to expect from children who came to buy an ice cream.
Most days we didn't mind their dithering, but on a busy day, it could try our
patience, with so many of them not being able to decide what they wanted,
and the queue growing longer behind them.

As I read the poem, I counted the number of Irish wildflower names the
poet had listed: there were 21 in all. I pointed out to my mum that we had
sold 21 flavours of ice cream in the shop. I also noted that the flowers named

all appeared to be associated in some way with Irish folklore medicinal herbal remedies. Was that just a coincidence, or me trying to find some sort of healing power in the words and names?

Michael Longley's little daughter, Sarah had added to the healing wreath of remembrance he had created in the poem, by spending her pocket money on carnations to lay outside the parlour in memory of my brother the week that he was killed. A little girl, in her childhood innocence, who saw John as simply the Ice Cream Man. She didn't see him as an off-duty policeman; someone to hate; someone who deserved to be killed. In her mind, she simply saw him as the Ice Cream Man and had been told that somebody had killed him. In fact, she probably thought it was me they killed, since I was the one she would usually have seen behind the counter each time she went into the parlour.

"Oh, I am so honoured to meet you," was Mr Longley's soft, gentle reply, as he took my hand and held it for what seemed like forever in the library-like silence that enveloped us both. He looked as if he had just found the one elusive book he had been searching for all his life. He was genuinely pleased that I had introduced myself. He said he treasured the letter my mother had written to him about "The Ice-Cream Man" elegy he had written about her son. He asked me how she was, and was saddened when I told him Mum had died.

"I am so sorry to hear that," he said, still holding my hand. "I have read and re-read her kind letter many times. It means a great deal to me."

I told him my mum was pleased he had written the elegy; that it had helped her believe that John would not be simply another statistic in our bloody, grubby catalogue of sectarian conflict and death. Someone cared about him being murdered, and had written a poem in his memory. To Mum, this meant John would not be easily forgotten, like so many others. He deserved better – all victims deserved better.

The warmth and compassion of the poet's handshake brought me a sense of peace that surprised me. I was glad I had spoken to him. He took out a notebook and asked if he could send me a copy of his new book, *Selected Poems*. I gave him my address and we said goodbye, with another warm handshake.

A few weeks later I received a copy of *Selected Poems* in the mail, as promised. On the inside cover was written: "For George Larmour – remembering the Ice Cream Man and the Ice Cream Man's mother"; it was signed "Michael Longley, 28–IV–99".

Stuffed inside the book, there was also a postcard. The image on it was a reproduction of a painting by Brian Ballard, *Poppies in White Jug*, painted in 1988 – ironically, the same year John was murdered. Again, I wondered if Michael had deliberately chosen a postcard, from so many available, which was so significant in terms of date, or was it just a coincidence? Or was there some other, unexplained power at work?

On the back of the postcard was the handwritten message:

Dear Mr Larmour,

It mattered a great deal to me that we were able to talk in Waterstones a few weeks ago. Here, as I promised, is my *Selected Poems*. The elegy for your brother is on p102. I would be grateful to learn more about your mother, who wrote me a beautiful, heartbreaking letter about the elegy.

Yours sincerely,

Michael Longley

Some years later, in 2006, I read a long article in the *Belfast Telegraph* featuring an interview with Michael Longley. One of the questions he was asked was if there were any taboo subjects in poetry. He answered "No", and went on to say: "Poetry should be able to deal with anything. There are subjects that are hugely difficult to write about, one being the suffering of fellow citizens when one wouldn't want to intrude or be impertinent. And yet it is important that one should write about that."

He continued: "One of the roles of the arts in a damaged society like ours is to remember the victims. Indeed, one of the most moving things that ever happened to me was when I wrote the poem 'The Ice-Cream Man'. He was murdered on the Lisburn Road. I got a letter from his mother. Under her name, she had printed: 'The Ice Cream Man's mother' – I treasure that letter." Michael also mentioned meeting me in Waterstones bookshop, and that I had introduced myself as "the Ice Cream Man's brother". He continued: "The fact that the whole family got something from my energy makes the whole enterprise worthwhile." He finished by saying that the treasured letter he had received from the Ice Cream Man's mother, and the letters he had received from other victims' family members, meant more to him than a hundred good critical reviews.

Michael Longley deserves those good critical reviews for the many poems he has written – but I can't thank him enough for caring about my brother and writing that one poem, which means so much to the Ice Cream Man's family.

Chapter Sixteen

Remembering Mr Hasty: 1974

Many of you reading my story will never have heard of Mr Jimmy Hasty. I had never heard of him either before 1974, when he touched my life. The letter I wrote to his wife on 4 April 2005, almost 31 years after that 1974 incident, explains how this happened:

Dear Mrs Hasty,

Please forgive me for this intrusion into your private life. I'm not even certain I have traced the right person, but I will hope to confirm this before handing you this letter. I have done a number of Internet searches, trying to trace you. I'm hoping I have managed to find the person I am looking for.

My name is George Larmour. I am 56 years old, and married with two daughters. I was born in the Shankill Road area of Belfast but have lived in Glengormley and Bangor most of my married life. My reason for trying to make contact is as follows:

In 1974 I was 25, married and living in Glengormley. I worked in the advertising department of the *Belfast Telegraph*, and my wife worked in Gallaher's, off Henry Street.

I always drove my wife to work each morning and then travelled on to the *Belfast Telegraph*. On the morning of 11 October 1974, I was, as usual, driving my wife to work. When we got to the corner of North Queen Street at just before 8.00 a.m., my wife said she heard what sounded like a shot or shots.

At the same time I noticed someone lying on the pavement on Brougham Street. I told my wife to get out of the car and walk on to her work, and I quickly drove on down Brougham Street to where the person was lying on the pavement.

I saw a man wearing a black leather jacket running back towards

North Queen Street, but the rest of Brougham Street was empty ... I stopped my car beside the person lying on the pavement and I saw that he was a man wearing work clothes. I think there was a small khaki or grey coloured duffle bag lying beside him.

Although there was no one else in the street, I immediately shouted out a number of times for someone to phone for an ambulance and police, and kneeled down beside the man to check how he was. He was still breathing but I did see that he was injured, and I assumed he had been shot.

I got two coats from my car and placed them over the man to try to keep him warm. I checked the pulse in his neck, which was weak but still there. I sat on the pavement beside him and held his head in my hands and continued to speak to him. I told him my name was George, and tried to reassure him that the ambulance was on its way and that I would stay with him. He was breathing very slowly and calmly. Although his eyes were closed most of the time and he didn't speak to me, he did open his eyes briefly when I spoke to him, and particularly when I asked if he could hear me.

I was aware of a woman who came out of her house beside us and another younger lady, who seemed to know something about first aid. They assured me that someone had phoned for an ambulance. It probably wasn't that long before the police arrived, but it seemed such a long time to me that morning, as I tried to keep talking to the man.

When the police arrived, the first policeman got down beside me and immediately said that the man was Jimmy Hasty, and indicated that he was a well-known local football champion who only had one arm. He seemed to know Mr Hasty and appeared upset at recognising him.

I wasn't even aware that the man on the pavement only had one arm, as I had covered him with the coats from my car, but the policeman lifted one of the coats and confirmed that ... it was indeed Jimmy Hasty.

I stayed with Mr Hasty and the policeman for a while but, as there was nothing more I could do, I suggested I leave the police to wait for the ambulance to arrive, and gave my name and contact details to them before travelling on to work.

It wasn't until about an hour later that the shock of what I had experienced hit me, and I broke down and cried in work, and had to go home. I suppose it was just the delayed reaction and at that stage I think someone from the newsroom had confirmed what I suppose I already knew: that Mr Hasty was dead. From subsequent news reports, I was aware that Mr Hasty had two young sons, Martin and Paul, and that his wife was called Margaret.

I felt so useless. There were times I often wondered if I should have tried to get him into my car and race to the Mater Hospital, instead of letting him lie there on the pavement until the ambulance arrived. Although the younger lady had suggested that it was probably best not to move him.

By the time I drove down Brougham Street that morning, it was completely empty – no cars or people, except for the man I mentioned I saw running back towards North Queen Street, wearing a leather jacket. However the police were able to confirm that this man had come forward and had been eliminated from their enquiries. The police asked me if I had seen any car or motorbike in the street, but I hadn't seen any vehicles.

Forgive me if this letter causes you unnecessary pain about what happened to your husband all those years ago. I have always thought I should have made contact with you to let you know what happened that morning. I just hope now it is not too late to bring you some small comfort, in knowing that Mr Hasty wasn't alone that morning of 11 October 1974.

I have some understanding of what your family has had to endure and the date of 11 October was to be of significance to me and my family many years after Mr Hasty's murder.

In July 1988 my wife and I opened a new ice cream parlour on the Lisburn Road called Barnam's World of Ice Cream … A few months after opening the parlour, I and my wife and daughters (aged 12 and 5) went off to Spain for a short holiday … However, while we were away, my brother John was shot and killed in the ice cream parlour. He was a member of the RUC but was off-duty that night and was doing me the favour of closing the parlour for me while we were on holiday. The night he was murdered was 11 October 1988, exactly 14 years after Mr Hasty was murdered.

My brother joining the RUC – it was his choice. I always thought he was mad for doing so. It was a thankless task, and eventually it cost him his life. There are many who will consider he deserved what he got, being a member of the RUC – I won't waste my time arguing with their interpretation. All I can look at is that he was my brother – nothing else – and I do still miss him to this day.

Although I was born on the Shankill Road, my mum and dad always brought us up to respect people as people and not for what religion they were. How sad that people can't live together and so much pain has been inflicted over the years so needlessly.

My mum and dad heard about my brother John's shooting on a newsflash on television. My dad got to the City Hospital before anyone else and he was allowed to identify my brother's body, with four bullet holes in it. This is something my dad never managed to get over and I watched him and Mum slowly die from broken hearts.

Dad was buried on the 11 October 1989, just one year after John's death. My mum, whose faith seemed to keep her going, found her own peace on the 1 September 1994, after years of pain at losing her son and husband.

On both occasions, I thankfully had the opportunity to be with my mum and dad when they died in the Mater Hospital. I wish so much that I had been able to speak to my brother when he died, but that was not to be. I can understand how you must feel, at not having had the chance to be with your husband during his final minutes on that morning in 1974.

Again, please forgive me if this letter causes you unnecessary pain and brings back memories of that awful day. I'm really unsure if I should even deliver this letter to you. I do hope that reading it helps in some small way to ease your pain, [in] knowing someone did care about Mr Hasty that morning in Brougham Street. I've never forgotten him.

Kind regards,

George Larmour

Chapter Seventeen

Meeting Mrs Hasty: 2005

When I knocked on the door that day in 2005 looking for Mrs Hasty, it was answered by a man who appeared to be in his late 50s or early 60s. I hesitated, as I wasn't expecting a man to answer the door. In my confusion I managed to ask if I had the correct address for a lady called Margaret Hasty, the wife of a Mr James Hasty.

It was then I heard a female voice from somewhere within the house asking, "Who is it, Jamesy?"

My mind went blank when I heard her call his name. James. Jimmy. Jamesy. The similarity threw me. I momentarily questioned if I had got this whole thing wrong, and had somehow mixed up the names in my search for this address.

Then the owner of the female voice was alongside the man on the doorstep, and she was asking if she could help me. She reminded me of my mother. A lovely lady, neatly dressed and holding her new husband, Jamesy's arm, as she curiously eyed me – a complete stranger on her doorstep, who was referring to her previous married name of Hasty.

When I confirmed that she was indeed the Margaret Hasty I was searching for, I explained that I wanted to give her a letter I had written about her husband, Mr Jimmy Hasty, who had been murdered in 1974. I was hoping I could simply hand the letter to her, return to my car and drive away. However this lovely lady asked me to come in, and took me through to a small living room at the back of the house, while her husband, Jamesy went into the other larger room at the front of the house.

She beckoned me to sit on the small sofa, and surprised me by joining me on it. There was no escaping the intimacy of the occasion now. Whether I wanted it or not, I had this lady's complete and undivided attention. So I started to tell her the story I had spent so long trying to put down on paper. For now, the letter stayed in my pocket.

I don't know when we held each other's hands. Maybe it was when I saw her first tears, which appeared very soon after I started talking to her. But for over an hour, I felt uneasy putting this lady through the obvious trauma of reliving her pain and the past, as I quietly tried to remember all the things I wanted to tell her.

I kept apologising, and saying that it might be easier if I just left her the letter. But she didn't want me to leave. Each time I felt things were getting too painful for her, she gently asked me to continue. She wanted to know every detail of every last moment of my time with Mr Hasty on that terrible morning in 1974.

When I had finally finished telling my story and she had no more questions, we instinctively hugged each other. It felt so natural. I desperately tried to hold back my own tears. I don't know why – I suppose I just didn't want to add my tears to her pain. We started our journey that day as strangers, but were now embracing like two old friends who had not seen each other for too many years.

Even in the warmth of that embrace, the memory of the coldness of that early morning pavement back in 1974 still haunted me that day. It had been too many years: why had I left it so long? It was the stark, cold fact of how much time had passed that kept troubling me at that moment; that had troubled me for so many years.

Was I afraid of getting involved in another unsolved murder? Or afraid to cross that invisible divide of tit-for-tat killings? And later, after John was killed, was I simply too busy with my own grief to care? Was I afraid of getting too close to someone else's pain? I don't know the answer. Maybe it was a mixture of all these reasons and more. Too many excuses are too easily brought out of the box and put back in again; it's easier to put things off for another day. But I knew I felt one thing for certain now: I should not have left it so long.

Instead of feeling glad that I had sought out this lady and finally spoken to her, I now felt ashamed at what I had done – or not done. For over 30 years, I had allowed her and her two young sons to grieve for James Hasty – her husband, their daddy – without them knowing the truth. For all that time, they might have been tormenting themselves about their loved one's final moments, with terrible images they had created in their own minds, based on the little knowledge they had. About how they had not been there to hold him, to comfort him and to tell him they loved him, as he lay dying on that cold pavement, callously shot as he walked to work and left to die by his heartless killers.

My story must have brought back many painful memories – sad, solitary memories that I know had never gone away for this lady and her sons. The flashbacks of that morning had never left me, a passing stranger who had not known James Hasty, so I could imagine how the unanswered questions must have burned deeply within his widow and her young sons over all those years.

"I am so sorry for not doing this sooner," I said again, and I begged her to forgive me. I could feel the weight of 30 years of guilt pressing heavily on my chest.

"There's nothing to forgive." She held my arm as she looked at me. "You have no idea how much you have changed my life today, Mr Larmour," she said in the softest of voices, a whisper almost. "To know that Jimmy didn't die alone that morning, that someone was with him, that someone cared for him and held him in those last minutes: that means everything to me."

There was a strange feeling in that small room that day. With each word she spoke, I could feel the pain lifting slightly from her and the guilt easing from me. Murder had managed to separate so many people throughout the years of the Troubles, but now somehow, murder had managed to bring us together.

Here we were, two people, one Protestant and one Catholic, who, through a simple circumstance of birth, were considered to be on opposite sides of the sectarian divide. One, whose husband was murdered on 11 October by Loyalist gunmen, for simply being a Catholic. I don't know the reasons why James Hasty's killers selected him. He was a Catholic who lived in the New Lodge area of Belfast, a well-known Republican area that was the stomping ground for some IRA members. And anyone who lived in that area must have been an IRA member or sympathiser: they were all the same, weren't they? And one whose brother, a policeman, was murdered on 11 October by IRA gunmen, simply for being a policeman. Whether he was a good and fair-minded policeman, serving all sections of his community no matter what their religion, or a bad, bigoted policeman – that wasn't important to his killers. They didn't bother checking his track record. Policeman were all the same, weren't they?

But people are not all the same, and that kind of excuse for killing someone is simply wrong. My brother wasn't a saint: he had many faults. I have no idea if he was a good or bad policeman. He certainly hated the IRA probably as much as they hated him. But killing your fellow man is simply wrong.

I hadn't known Mr Hasty, but his wife Margaret assured me that he had been a hard-working, ordinary man who would never have hurt anyone. He was in no way connected to any illegal paramilitary organisation, and only cared for his wife and two young sons. I had never even considered whether or not Mr Hasty was involved in any paramilitary activity. I just knew that his murder was something that had affected me personally that morning, and ever since. I had watched another human being die as I held him on a cold pavement all those years ago, and the memory of those traumatic final moments never left me.

In 2015, a recent Radio Ulster documentary, "Diamond in the Rough", charted the footballing history of Mr Hasty. Maybe one day someone will pay tribute to his life and memory, and write the life story of this forgotten Belfast football legend. It's a story that deserves to be told, not just in written form but on the big screen also. With many parallels to the movie *Cinderella Man*, which was a tribute to legendary boxer, James J Braddock, the story of Jimmy Hasty is of someone with the same characteristics of courage, grit and down-to-earth decency. At times when most people branded him a loser with a broken hand, James Braddock fought and beat many tough opponents in the ring. But the love of a family and a determination to succeed can overcome any disability.

Disability didn't stop Jimmy Hasty, either. As a young lad of 14 years of age, he started his very first job in Belfast. But that fateful first day in the job saw him losing his left arm when it was caught in a works machine. However Jimmy Hasty didn't let that terrible incident ruin his life, and despite losing his arm, he went on to become a great football player.

On occasion perhaps, out of some sort of misguided sympathy, defenders backed off a bit more when they saw the one-armed striker racing towards them with the ball at his feet. If they did, they paid dearly for their lack of judgement. Jimmy Hasty would duck and weave around them without losing his balance, his empty left sleeve waving to them as he sailed past them, to put the ball firmly in the back of their net, yet again. When necessary, he would use what remained of his left arm stump to cleverly lean on them in a tackle. When defenders would call to the referee for a foul, their protests were in vain. How could a referee book Jimmy for supposedly pushing a defender off the ball, when he didn't even have an arm? The talented young player used that natural skill and unique tackling ability to score over 100 goals in matches across Ireland in the early 1960s.

Many people knew the one-armed footballer during those years in the 1960s and 1970s: he was so easy to pick out, with that empty sleeve hanging by his side. Perhaps that's what made it simple for his killers to target him, that morning of 11 October 1974 as he walked down Brougham Street on his way to work to support his young family.

Not long after my visit, I received a card and letter from Mrs Hasty. In it, she explained how pleased she was that I had decided to find her and write her the letter, and that I had personally spent the time telling her my memories of that morning in 1974. She told me that my letter and the fact of me getting in touch with her had surely made life a bit better after so many years.

Just like my "swalley water" lifeguard, and my dad and his friend, John McCann at Dunkirk, I didn't hesitate that morning in 1974. I held Mr Hasty as he died and I told him I cared about him, a fellow human being. Although I obviously wish I hadn't hesitated for so long, I am glad that I found Mrs Hasty and brought her some small comfort, which she so much deserved – even though it was many years too late. I'm not a religious person, but I hope, if there is somewhere we all end up after we die, that my dad, my mum, my brother, John McCann and Mr Hasty are all there now, enjoying each other's company and proving that those who wanted to separate them in life simply because of their different religions, didn't succeed in doing so in their deaths.

Chapter Eighteen

Unfinished Business: October 2002

I spent the evening of 2 October 2002 alone at home. My wife and daughters were, sensibly, off out doing something more important with their lives, rather than sitting like I was, in front of the "box", watching the usual movie repeats or an episode of the new breed of cheaply-produced reality television programmes.

I had tried to read a book earlier, but it wasn't great, so I switched on the TV, and flicked through the paper to see what was on. At 9.00 pm there was a programme called "Wild Weather", which entailed journalist, Donal MacIntyre visiting the wettest places on earth. I wondered if he was going to include Ireland in his travels. We always like to moan about our wet weather here. I suppose there has to be some payback for those forty shades of green this island is famous for.

But no, there Donal was in the Norwegian city of Bergen, where it rains on average 265 days of the year. Then he was in India, going on about the fact that during the monsoon period, they estimate that 25 billion tons of water – yes, 25 billion! – falls each day. That's one hell of a lot of rain! And we have the cheek to complain about the odd wet day here in Royal Avenue. God, we don't know we're living.

At the end of the programme, I was ready for an early night, but a trailer for another programme caught my attention, and I decided to stay up to watch it. "Unfinished Business" was a documentary profiling Professor Jack Crane, the State Pathologist for Northern Ireland, whose job it was to establish the exact cause of death in cases of apparent murder, suicide, accident and unexplained natural fatalities. I was already aware that Professor Crane's work had involved him in some of the worst incidents of the Troubles in Northern Ireland, including the Omagh and Enniskillen bombings, and that his expertise had been called upon also in relation to the Bosnia and Kosovo conflicts, where he has investigated war crimes on behalf of the United Nations. So I settled down to watch what I expected would be a fascinating, although perhaps disturbing, programme but one that would naturally be of interest to me, given our family's experience of John's murder.

At the outset of the documentary, Professor Crane said that every dead body had something to tell him. He indicated that he carried out around 1,500 autopsies annually – that is a lot of dead people talking to him every year, I reflected! He said that he had no difficulty dealing with dead bodies; that he had a job to do and he just had to get on with it. But he admitted he had been face-to-face with some of the worst atrocities of Northern Ireland's Troubles, and that he was always acutely aware that with every dead body that was presented to him for an autopsy, there was a family grieving.

The professor suggested that, to help him establish the cause of death, particularly when someone has been shot, it is crucially important to get X-rays done. He then held up an X-ray of the victim of a fatal, terrorism-related shooting. He said that the person had been shot a number of times, with perhaps four bullets in total – but that only one of these bullets was responsible for the person's death. At this, I turned the sound up and stared at the X-ray being shown on the TV screen.

Professor Crane went on to point out that the person could easily have survived a number of the bullets, but that there had been one significant bullet which caused their death. By this time, I was convinced I was looking at my brother John's X-ray. I already knew he had been shot four times, and that only one of the bullets had killed him: the one that entered his left shoulder and travelled through his neck and spinal cord, before lodging in his right shoulder. Now I was watching without really listening. All I could think about was the X-ray I had just seen Professor Crane show on screen. In fact I would hold that troubling image in my mind for the following nine or ten years. It disturbed and disquieted me greatly.

I only finally got the courage to write to Professor Jack Crane a few years ago. In my letter, I asked him if he would be willing to tell me if the X-ray he used as an illustration in the 2002 programme, "Unfinished Business" was in fact of my brother, John. I should have written to him sooner, but grief is a strange companion. It clouds your judgement and conjures up unnecessary pain.

It took Professor Crane a few weeks to reply. As he later explained, the delay was due to him having to check his files and the content of the programme. He was now able to confirm that the X-ray I had seen on screen that night in 2002 was not of John.

I cried that night in 2002, when I saw an X-ray on screen that I was sure was of my brother and of the bullet that killed him. And I cried again when I got the letter from Professor Crane, telling me that I was wrong in my assumption.

All these years later, am I glad now that I was wrong? Yes, I suppose I am. But that X-ray was very compelling proof of Professor Crane's point – that there's a very fine line between life and death. If luck had been on their side, the person whose X-ray Professor Crane showed on screen could quite easily still be alive today, as could my brother John. They were both hit a number of times with bullets that someone hoped would kill them. Most of those bullets were redundant and didn't achieve their killer's objective, but in my brother's case and that of the unidentified victim of the programme, all it took was one single bullet to deprive each of them of life.

Because of hatred or sectarian bigotry, coupled with a degree of bad luck, my brother John and that person, whose identity will forever remain a mystery to me, are dead. What a waste!

Chapter Nineteen

Blair's Weasel Words

There were many times during the years following John's death that I became angry and frustrated. Sometimes an incident would bring the memories, the grief and the trauma flooding back – and with this, my anger that my brother had been murdered and his killers had still not been brought to justice. More often however it was the patronising comments from politicians over the years which would be the source of my frustration.

On one such occasion, I was prompted to write an open letter to Prime Minister Tony Blair, to tell him what I really thought about him and his "phoney Tony" sincerity. My letter was published in the *Belfast Telegraph* just before Christmas, on 17 December 2004:

> I suppose I should thank Prime Minister Tony Blair for making every Christmas so memorable for all the victims of terrorism here. I [am] one of those victims' family members he seemed to care so much about. That special time of year again, with all the shopping, the presents under the tree, the festivities, too much wine and lots of turkey, not forgetting the empty chairs around the table on Christmas Day. And of course . . . that time again for another of Mr Blair's really catchy soundbites.
>
> What would Christmas have been without them? I remember the one about "the writing's on the wall", when he made the pledge to sort out terrorism, and he even signed the big poster in front of the cameras to prove how genuine he was. That was really clever. Then there was, "the train's leaving the station and everyone better get on board". That was sheer magic. That was the year everyone was wondering if we would see a photograph of all the weapons that were supposed to be decommissioned. I visualised the Polar – or should that be the 'Polaroid' – Express racing out of Central Station, with Tony Blair sounding the whistle as Gerry Adams and

Ian Paisley raced up the platform, trying to jump on board before it was too late. What a picture! I don't think the train ever left the station that year, and we never did get a Polaroid of the mountain of weapons supposedly put beyond use.

But Mr Blair's best soundbite was the one he delivered with such sincerity in the Waterfront Hall one Christmas time. It was pure genius. He really had a way with words, and his clasped hands and pauses just added so much to the story. It was the one about the weary traveller, the mountain climber trudging all the way along the path and how, just when he thinks he's at the peak, there before him is another small mound, which he still has to get over. It was intended to convey his determination to keep going in pursuit of his goal, no matter how many hills there were to climb. Such inner strength; such determination. What a story! I could almost feel my weary knees ache as I visualised that image in my head.

Unfortunately, I was already familiar with that story. I was just one of the many who could recall it. Weary travellers, all of us, who trudged the same path every week to that small mound of earth that we could never get over, no matter how much we tried. It was that small mound of earth which was disgracefully trampled over in the name of appeasement. That small mound, where our loved ones lay buried, murdered by the terrorists Mr Blair so warmly welcomed into his Downing Street home. That small mound, where we gently laid our holly wreaths on Christmas Day, and told those we missed so much that we had not forgotten them…

I'm sure even Mr Blair's friend, Bertie Ahern, could visualise Mrs McCabe, whose husband, Garda Gerry McCabe was murdered, visiting that Christmas her husband's small mound of earth – the one she would never get over.

We had to keep going, Mr Blair, despite our grief and your patronising media soundbites. Our families needed us to stay strong and determined. We were weary. Tired of hearing phrases and words that sounded good but meant so little. Tired of being sidelined as long as the wrongdoers in our midst were kept happy. Tired of elected politicians picking up their pay cheques for behaving like schoolchildren. Tired listening to endless promises and clever stories at Christmas that didn't make life any better, Mr Blair.

I don't know if Prime Minister Blair ever read my open letter to him. If he did, he never bothered to reply. Perhaps he was too busy conjuring up his next hand-wringing, "hand-of-history" soundbite to care about some dead guy's brother.

§

Just a matter of weeks after this, in the final days of January 2005, news of the brutal murder of someone else's brother in Belfast compelled me to put pen to paper again, and send another letter to the *Belfast Telegraph*. After a quarrel in a bar, Robert McCartney had been knifed to death on the street outside by members of the IRA; another man with him was also wounded. Because of campaigning by Robert's sisters, the case would be reported and discussed around the world; even the US president knew about Robert McCartney.

I was aware that my letter needed to be carefully constructed and sensitively worded, so that I would not cause offence to the grieving family. I sincerely hope it didn't cause any upset.

> I understand fully the pain Robert McCartney's sisters are experiencing – the grief mixed with anger, at seeing his killers shielded from justice. My brother was also butchered in cold blood by IRA killers when he, too, was unarmed and defenceless. So why is his death so different?
>
> No matter how I word this article, I am sure it will be interpreted by some – for their own gain – as causing offence to the sisters and family of Robert McCartney. That is not my intention, and I apologise in advance if that occurs. I do not wish to add to their suffering and pain. I admire the courage and conviction of Robert McCartney's sisters, in trying to seek justice for a brother they obviously adored and loved, and miss so much. I support them in their quest for truth.
>
> I understand fully the pain they are experiencing and the range of emotions that are filling their days and long, dark, lonely nights … I know because my own brother was also murdered by the IRA, and his evil killers have never been brought to justice.
>
> Of course, my brother was one of the IRA's "legitimate targets", because he was a member of the RUC. His murder was just

another statistic, easily forgotten. None of his IRA killers were ostracised by Sinn Féin voters in Republican areas. In fact, some even rejoiced at the news of his murder. My brother was murdered while off-duty … Outnumbered and given no chance to survive, just like Robert McCartney.

Is my brother's murder so different from Robert's because John was a policeman and deserved to be killed? Did being a member of the RUC make my brother's murder more acceptable to the people who voted for Sinn Féin? Was it the fact that he was murdered by trained killers, fighting a supposed legitimate war on behalf of a mandate, that made it okay?

Did the phrase "the Armalite and the ballot box" have a patriotic ring to it that is more acceptable to Sinn Féin voters? Whereas "a carving knife and a ballot box" wouldn't confer the same sense of authority to the freedom fighter's cause?

It is nauseating to watch Sinn Féin/IRA spokespersons refusing to fully support Robert's sisters. Their weasel words prolong the agony for a family who cannot come to terms with their grief until justice is done in court.

The IRA have "expelled" three of their trained killers, as if they are simply schoolyard bullies who stepped out of line and deserve detention or suspension. The daily news shows Sinn Féin/IRA godfathers squirming because the killer robots of the IRA, that they helped to perfect over the past 30 years, are starting to malfunction and kill the wrong people – their own people. That was not supposed to happen.

I listen to Gerry Adams and Martin McGuinness suggesting that Robert's killers should do the patriotic thing and be answerable for their actions. But even that smacks of propaganda. Are Robert's killers to be given honourable, heroic status for coming forward?

As in all walks of life, there are good and bad apples on all sides. I accept there were rogue cops in the RUC who tarnished the image of the police. Many Catholics died needlessly at the hands of Loyalists, and many Protestants died needlessly at the hands of Republican paramilitaries. Not everyone voted for violence when they voted for Sinn Féin or Loyalist parties; many voted for peace, in the hope that our children would have a better life.

All violent deaths are senseless. There had to be a better way. My brother's death ... didn't advance the Peace Process or achieve a united Ireland. It only achieved heartache for those left behind, who had to pick up the pieces of their shattered lives. It was, like all the other violent deaths, simply a waste of a life.

I sincerely hope Robert McCartney's sisters and family get the justice they seek and deserve, and that he is not forgotten like so many others. I hope also that his family get some comfort from the outpouring of support from all sections of our divided community. I hope his death will bring about change, and that we can rid our communities of the swaggering gangsters and drug dealers who poison our children.

I hope those we elect get the message that they cannot ride roughshod over our emotions and that our vote cannot be abused. We can vote for someone else.

Sadly of course people didn't vote for someone else. The same tribal politics prevail to this day.

Chapter Twenty

The Browning 9 mm

In the course of my research for this book, a routine internet search for "1988 Troubles' incidents" brings up a familiar photograph on my computer screen. It's black and white. I've seen it before many times, but it's much larger now on this screen than the previous versions I have viewed. I'm not the only one who has seen this image. By now, 27 years after it first appeared on our television screens and in newspapers and magazines, as well as, in later years, on the internet, it has probably been viewed by millions of people worldwide. It is very likely that you will have seen it too. It's an image that does not fade with the passing of time. And it has haunted me for the past 27 years.

The photographer that day captured forever a moment in time that brings back the events of a horrific day in Belfast in the late 1980s. The first time I saw it, probably like everyone else, I viewed this picture with morbid curiosity. I didn't realise then that it would come to mean so much to me, just a few months after it was taken. And that, as the years passed and my own investigations into John's murder continued, it would take on an ever more sinister significance.

The photo shows a side-on view of a car, with a crowd of people behind it. There's a man's face staring out of the smashed window on the driver's side. His left hand is clutching the side of the window frame, as if steadying himself for his next move. In his right hand he holds his regulation Browning 9 mm gun, and he appears to be staring straight at the camera. His face is in shadow just inside the car, but I can make out his dark hair and moustache. And unmistakable too is the expression on his face – a look of determination mixed with a sense of inevitability that is all the more distressing to look at, because we all know the outcome for him.

The date is 19 March 1988, just six months before my brother John will be murdered. The man in the car is Corporal Derek Wood. Staring at the image, I look intently behind Corporal Wood. For, although I can't see him in the photograph, I know that in the passenger's seat beside Wood is 23-year-old Corporal David Howes.

The photograph makes Derek Wood look older than his 24 years. Although dressed in casual civilian clothing, both young men are members of the Signals Regiment of the British Army, based in Northern Ireland. At this moment they have found themselves surrounded by mourners at the funeral in West Belfast of IRA member, Kevin Brady, who died during Michael Stone's attack on mourners in Milltown Cemetery earlier that week.

The Brady funeral was moving along the Andersonstown Road towards the burial plot in Milltown Cemetery, when Corporal Wood's silver Volkswagen Passat appeared from nowhere, travelling at high speed towards the front of the cortège. The car mounted a pavement, causing panic among the mourners, who started to scatter in different directions.

After regaining control of the car and turning into a side street, Corporal Derek Wood found his path blocked. He tried to reverse out of the street again but his way was barred by black taxis attending the funeral. The two soldiers were now surrounded by dozens of the mourners, who started to attack the car – some with their fists, others with a stepladder and wheel brace. They quickly managed to smash the car's side windows.

It was then that Derek Wood produced his gun at the window, in an attempt to keep the crowd at bay. He fired a single warning shot into the air, which made the crowd briefly scatter. But soon he and his colleague were overpowered and dragged from the car. They were taken to one side, and stripped, questioned and beaten. Then they were bundled into one of the black taxis and driven to waste ground, behind a row of shops in the area. They were finally shot dead with Derek Wood's own pistol – the one I am looking at now again in the photograph; the one he is holding in his hand as he stares through the smashed car window.

Why were the two British soldiers there that day? Was it their own morbid curiosity at wanting to witness an IRA funeral? Or were they on some kind of official covert duty in the area? No proper explanation has ever been given by the Army, as to why Corporals Derek Wood and David Howes should be driving through a staunchly Republican area of West Belfast on the day of an IRA funeral. Perhaps we will never know the real reason. It could be that there wasn't any sensible reason for their presence that day.

Tensions were already running high at that time, following the deaths on 6 March in Gibraltar of Mairéad Farrell, Sean Savage and Daniel McCann, and the attack by Michael Stone in Milltown Cemetery on 16 March, when Kevin Brady had been killed. So the sudden appearance of Wood and Howes must have looked to those present like the beginning of another attack on a high-profile Republican funeral, which was enough for the crowd to descend like locusts on their car. The young soldiers' fate was sealed; there was no escape for them.

The IRA kept Derek Wood's Browning 9 mm, passed on to them after the murder of the two corporals. They would use it a matter of months later, on 2 August 1988, when they killed UDR Lance Corporal Roy Butler in the Park Shopping Centre in West Belfast. The lance corporal from Newtownabbey was off-duty that day, and he was shot dead in front of his family inside the centre, as he emerged from one of the shops. At his inquest it was confirmed that of dozens of witnesses who saw the two unmasked gunmen shoot him, none had come forward to provide police with any information.

And once again, a few months after that, the IRA brought the Browning out of its hiding place again. This time the gunman, who guarded the door in Barnam's World of Ice Cream that night of 11 October 1988, used it to shoot two innocent teenagers who made the mistake of loving our ice cream too much. Apparently that was a good enough excuse in 1988 for the IRA to shoot you.

Therefore, within the space of about seven months in 1988, Corporal Wood's Browning was used in connection with four murders – those of both Corporals, of Roy Butler and of my brother John. All four victims in these attacks were in civilian clothes, and effectively off-duty from their security jobs. And the IRA had further plans for that special Browning. As we will see in a later chapter, it would be taken from Northern Ireland to Europe by an IRA active service team to wreak further suffering and spill more blood in their quest for the unification of Ireland. It would eventually be recovered, along with other weapons, in Germany by the authorities there on 2 June 1992, following the murder of Major Mike Dillon-Lee and the arrests of known Irish Republicans, Donna Maguire, Gerard Harte, Sean Hick and Paul Hughes.

Chapter Twenty-One

Destroying Evidence

I was first introduced to the workings of the Historical Enquiries Team (HET) in 2007, when I was handed a glossy brochure entitled, "Policing the Past – Introducing the Work of the Historical Enquiries Team". They had taken over responsibility from the Serious Crime Review Branch of the PSNI for the cold case re-investigation into John's murder.

For reasons that will become apparent in the following chapters, I reread that brochure many times during the period I had dealings with the HET. Having been involved in the advertising and printing industry, I have to admit to admiring the design and layout of this publication, as well as the clever copywriting. Taken together, it all gave the strong impression that this was an organisation which would deal with victims' families professionally and meticulously, and endeavour to provide them with the truth – and with this, some kind of closure. Sadly, on reflection and after years of frustration, I can only say now that, for me, their work didn't live up to their promises. In relation to our family and John's murder, they sadly did not fulfill either of their main objectives, as set out so confidently on the first page of that glossy brochure:

The HET: Our Role
We envisage a re-examination process for all deaths attributable to the security situation, with case reviews leading to re-investigation in appropriate circumstances where there are evidential opportunities.

Families will sit at the very heart of our investigations. The primary objective will be to work with them to achieve a measure of resolution in these difficult cases. We do not underestimate the complexity of this challenge. Nor do we underestimate the potential emotional stress for relatives attached to re-visiting these tragic events. It is for this reason that our Family Liaison section will have a central role in our work.

The second objective will be to enable a sense of confidence among those directly affected and the wider public, that all these cases will be comprehensively examined to current professional standards, to the extent that as an organisation, we can be satisfied that all evidential possibilities have been explored.

§

I had in fact been made aware of the connection between Derek Wood's Browning and the attack in Barnam's not long after my brother's murder. So, every time that dramatic and disturbing news footage of the two corporals would be re-run on our television screens, or the story would appear in local newspapers or magazines, usually accompanied by that haunting black-and-white photograph, I would be aware of its significance for my own family and for other families. Families who, although they have never met, are connected in a circle of grief because of the murder of their loved ones.

In late 2007, when the Historical Enquiries Team started their cold case review into John's murder, one of the first facts I asked them to confirm was the connection between the attack at Barnam's and the Browning 9 mm. I wanted to have it officially acknowledged that the Browning belonging to Derek Wood, seen by millions of people all over the world, was the same gun that was used in Barnam's that night.

The first HET report did not however confirm this fact. I rejected its conclusions, demanding that they tell me the truth, which, eventually, they did. Did the IRA deliberately choose to use Corporal Derek Wood's Browning 9 mm when they came to kill my brother that night? I can only speculate, but it seems likely that they did, because they wanted the police to know that they still had the gun, and that they intended to use it to kill as many army and police personnel as possible, in some sort of twisted revenge scenario. They knew that each time they used it, ballistics evidence gathered in the follow-up investigations would prove it was the same Browning. Again, I can only assume that is also the reason why the IRA decided to take this weapon with them to Europe, when they extended their campaign of murder to Holland and Germany in 1990.

The fact is however that in 2008, the Historical Enquiries Team were completely unaware of the whereabouts of Derek Wood's Browning. They knew it had been recovered in Germany in 1990 – but that was the extent of their knowledge and they were, it seemed, perfectly happy to leave it at that. It was in fact John's son, my nephew Gavin, who tracked down this weapon. Through his own exhaustive investigations into his dad's murder, Gavin was able to tell the Historical Enquiries Team that Corporal Wood's Browning was still in Germany.

I personally was appalled when I learned this news. I would have thought such a significant weapon would have been of interest to the RUC in Belfast in 1992, when it was first recovered in Germany. I would have expected them to apply for its return to Belfast for proper forensic analysis, and to be put into secure evidential storage here. The RUC would have known the significance of that Browning 9 mm, which was seen in television news footage worldwide. They would also have known that it was forensically connected through official test fire results to at least three murders and two attempted murders, here in Northern Ireland.

If I thought this was shocking and a dereliction of duty, I would soon be even more dismayed, when in 2008 I insisted that the HET bring the Browning back from Germany. I demanded that they apply to the German authorities to have the gun released into HET custody, so that even many years too late, it could be forensically tested for any potential evidential opportunity in regard to the attack in Barnam's. I also felt that the families of the victims who were killed with that Browning might also feel as I did. As stated in their glossy brochure, one of the chief aims of the HET was to pursue any possible evidential opportunities to provide victims' families with the truth.

When, in 2009, I received the HET's follow-up report, I had to re-read the section that dealt with the Browning a number of times. I simply couldn't believe what I was seeing, officially and in print, in a cold case review report:

> The HET has established the Browning is currently held in the training department of the Federal Police in Germany. It has been regularly stripped down, reassembled and cleaned for training purposes. The HET has assessed the likelihood of any forensic evidence being retrieved as negligible, and has therefore decided not to pursue recovery of the weapon.

To think that such a significant weapon – which the police in Germany and Belfast know belonged to Corporal Derek Wood – has been used over many years to train rookie police officers in Germany in how to dismantle and reassemble a Browning, is utterly breathtaking. They know that this gun was used in the murders of Woods and Howes, that it was used in Roy Butler's murder, and that it was used in the fatal attack on my brother John; they also know that it was taken to Europe by the IRA to inflict further mayhem there. But it has never occurred to them to try to preserve the evidential integrity of the weapon.

All potential evidence was of course destroyed when the German police authorities, for whatever reason, allowed this significant murder weapon, that they themselves must have seen in that haunting black-and-white photograph of Corporal Wood, to be taken out of its evidence bag, and cleaned and stripped down by hundreds of new police recruits as part of their in-house training. It is an appalling fact and a disgrace. When we consider that, because of advances in DNA technology, successful convictions in historical murder investigations have been secured even many years after the event, it is scandalous that this murder weapon has been evidentially destroyed. Perhaps the German police made their decision based on the level of disinterest shown by the RUC, in not requesting its return to Belfast?

The current Chief Constable of the PSNI, Mr George Hamilton, should request that the Browning 9 mm be brought back to Belfast without delay – if for no other reason than that it is an insult, to the memory of those it was used to kill and to their families, that it should be casually used for routine training. Furthermore, the British government should demand that someone within the German government issue an apology for allowing a murder weapon in their care to be used as a training weapon. And they should also apologise for thereby allowing the destruction of potential evidence.

Chapter Twenty-Two

The Speed Six Ruger

The other gun used in the attack in Barnam's World of Ice Cream was a Speed Six Ruger Magnum Revolver: this was the weapon used to murder my brother. Cross-referenced ballistic evidence would show that this gun was used in three other murders. It was used on 9 September 1988, a few weeks before John's murder, to kill 29-year-old Colin Abernethy on the train at Finaghy, as he travelled from his home in Lisburn to work at the Northern Ireland Electricity headquarters in Belfast. It was then used again in Roermond, Holland on 27 May 1990, when an active service unit of the IRA killed two Australian tourists, Stephen Melrose and Nick Spanos.

The Ruger was recovered in Belgium a few weeks later. The original manufacturer's serial number had been expertly removed from it: someone at some stage had clearly wished to conceal the identity of the original source of this weapon. I was keen to find out why. It was my belief in fact that this was not just any Ruger, but a police-issue weapon originally owned by the Royal Ulster Constabulary.

Once more, in 2007 and 2008, the HET didn't know the whereabouts of the Ruger. Credit for providing that information must go again to John's son, my nephew, Gavin. Without his persistent and professional investigative efforts, the HET might never have found it. Gavin discovered that the Ruger was lying in an evidence bag in police headquarters in Belgium, and that it had lain there in storage since 1990. It seemed that the official body – set up in Northern Ireland, using millions of pounds of taxpayers' money, to carry out cold case reviews of the many unsolved murders during our so-called Troubles – had to be told by a victim's family member where to look for a murder weapon.

As with the fate of the Browning, the fact that the Ruger, which was known to have been connected in at least two murders here in Belfast, was allowed to lie in storage for so many years in Belgium, is appalling. The RUC at the time should have been keen to bring it back to Belfast as soon as possible, for additional forensic analysis relating to the two murders here. But they didn't. No one here in Belfast was interested in testing that murder weapon in 1990, or at any other time since then. I wondered why.

In 2008 therefore, I demanded that the HET bring the Ruger back to Northern Ireland for forensic examination and in particular, Low Copy Number DNA analysis. After weeks of deliberation, during which they suggested that the Ruger might not have been stored in proper forensic conditions during the previous 20-odd years, the HET finally agreed to my request. In 2009, members of the Historical Enquiries Team travelled to Belgium and finally brought the Ruger back to Northern Ireland. I was, naturally, pleased with this result. But I was under no illusions as to how many more months of protracted efforts would be required on my part, to ensure that things would be taken to the next stage.

Chapter Twenty-Three

Protecting the Past

On the 20th anniversary of John's murder in 2008, I decided to write another open letter, this time to deputy First Minister, Martin McGuinness, which was published in the local morning newspaper, the *News Letter.* As well as setting out the background to John's murder and something of its aftermath in the intervening years, in this letter I took the opportunity to convey what my experiences with the HET had been like thus far, as well as my profound scepticism about their ability to deliver on the objectives they had so clearly set themselves:

> … The murder of my brother [by the IRA] didn't achieve anything but heartache for those left behind, who are still picking up the pieces of their shattered lives 20 years later.
>
> The two gunmen who pulled the triggers that night have never been convicted of his murder. They can't be named. Their identities have to be protected. I wonder why? The initial police investigation was, for whatever reason, not given the care and attention it deserved. Were [those investigating] just incompetent – or was there something or someone to hide?
>
> During the past year the Historical Enquiries Team carried out a cold case review of my brother's murder, which concluded with a report that I could have written myself many years ago. It told me nothing I didn't already know. It was an academic, meaningless report that proved to me that this new HET [initiative] is a cynical, costly, manipulative exercise in victim management, designed to make it appear that someone really gives a damn. [My brother's murder was] another case reviewed without any result, and hopefully stored away and forgotten. Just another file in the pile of 3,268 files on their desks.
>
> I cooperated with the HET for over a year. My initial contact,

who was seconded from England, showed understanding and empathy with my concerns but couldn't provide me with the answers I wanted. She recommended fresh arrests be made, but was overruled. I learned of her departure from the HET by letter.

Her replacement, also from England, made contact with me once and appeared to know little about the case. When I telephoned to speak to her in March of this year, I was told she too had left the HET and returned to England. So much for those all-important family members being kept informed.

I don't blame these two individuals. Their hands were tied. Their superiors make the real decisions and in most cases, [the upshot of] those decisions is that nothing will be done to bring the perpetrators to justice anyway. Not one known suspect – or, in the HET's jargon, "person of interest" – named in my brother's original investigation files was arrested and interviewed as part of their cold case review. The final HET report was meant to bring resolution and hopefully some measure of closure. It didn't.

If this is an example of what most victims' families have to look forward to at the end of their cooperation with the HET, then I sincerely hope they are prepared for major disappointment. Mr David Cox, the head of the HET, should make it clear publicly to all those families that are still waiting, that it is unlikely anyone will be brought to justice for the murder of their loved ones. Indeed, it is unlikely any "persons of interest" will be even interviewed under caution. In my experience, that is the simple truth.

The Chief Constable, Sir Hugh Orde appears frustrated by the time it is taking to "police the past". He wants to get on with dealing with the present. Understandable, I suppose – but what he doesn't seem to fully understand is that it is our lives he is dealing with. Unfortunately most victims' families don't have the luxury of simply forgetting the past: it is with us every day.

The dust on my brother's file has been briefly blown away, but after almost 20 years, his murder is still unsolved. Do we not have the right to ask why? And to ask, what is the point of having the Historical Enquiries Team, if they are unable or unwilling to arrest and question known suspects as part of their in-depth review?

I was glad to hear deputy First Minister, Martin McGuinness

quite rightly recently condemning the attempted murder of another police officer near Castlederg. He and his Sinn Féin members have called on people to come forward to the police with any information they have that will help catch those responsible.

Dare I ask him to do the same for my brother? Will he publicly call on people to come forward and give the necessary information which will expose my brother's killers – his former comrades in the IRA who helped pave that long, bloody, headstoned road he trod to Stormont? Or is protecting them – and himself – from the past more important?

The Ice Cream Man's Brother

I assumed Martin McGuinness might have been too busy dealing with his ministerial duties to have read my open letter in the *News Letter*, so I sent a personal copy of my published letter directly to the deputy First Minister at Stormont. I never received any private or public reply.

Chapter Twenty-Four

Eames/Bradley

Towards the end of January 2009, the bombshell revelation was leaked that, among the recommendations of the soon-to-be published report of the Eames/Bradley Consultative Group on the Past, was a proposal that a "recognition payment" of £12,000 should be made to all families – security forces, republican, loyalist and other – who had lost a loved one in the Northern Ireland conflict, irrespective of whether the victim was a perpetrator who had died during an incident they were involved in, or a policeman or soldier, or an innocent bystander caught up in violence because they happened to be in the wrong place at the wrong time.

Like many other people from affected families, I was outraged by this proposal. Once more, I felt compelled to give voice to my feelings in yet another letter to the press. Entitled "Payout would be a Betrayal", and printed alongside a newspaper cartoonist's depiction of Lord Eames opening a can of worms, my letter was published in the *Belfast Telegraph* just after the release of the Eames/Bradley report:

> The proposal from Lord Eames and Denis Bradley is disgraceful, and can only be described as the ultimate betrayal of the innocent men, women and children who were mercilessly murdered.
>
> Having my own RUC brother murdered at the hands of IRA killers and having seen my mum and dad die prematurely as a result of their grief, I fully understand everyone's tears are the same. I am sure the mother of a dead terrorist sheds those same bitter tears, year after year. I have no argument with her. But for two intelligent and supposedly compassionate people to come up with such a "one payment fits all" suggestion, after 19 months of careful deliberation and consultation with many victims' groups, is truly breathtaking. Do they really expect a £12,000 "sweetener" will help victims' families come to terms with their grief? Do they

really think that is what victims' families want, after their years of pain and loss? Do they really have any idea how hurtful such a proposal is to victims' families?

I don't want your £12,000, Lord Eames. Some of us can't be bought off that easily. I don't want patronising academic reports and disgraceful proposals, Mr Bradley. Or pointless investigations by bodies such as the Historical Enquiries Team, who, despite knowing the names of my brother's killers, never even questioned them as part of their supposed in-depth cold case investigation. I simply want the truth. I only speak for myself. I'm sure others will have a different view on your proposal.

George Larmour

I never heard from Lord Eames nor Denis Bradley. Perhaps they didn't feel it was a matter of sufficient importance to make the effort to contact me and to discuss my views in greater depth.

Chapter Twenty-Five

The Search for DNA

Forensic investigation techniques have advanced greatly since John was murdered in 1988. The ever-growing popularity in recent times of television and film police dramas and true crime documentaries, has meant that we are all wiser, more expert armchair detectives – or at least that even the layman now has some insight into what modern forensics have made possible. Crimes seem to be solved so easily, in the two hours it takes for us to sit through yet another Hollywood thriller. CCTV images now capture our every movement. News reports show grainy images of a possible killer stalking his latest victim, as she casually shops in a local supermarket before meeting her fate at his evil hands. And we have all by now become accustomed to hearing those "smoking gun" initials in the vocabulary of crime-solving: DNA – or Deoxyribonucleic acid, to give it its full scientific name.

Without getting too technical (basically because I don't understand the science anyway), it has been established that every one of us on this planet has a unique DNA, which makes up the cells in our body. This dictates what colour our eyes are and what blood group we are, amongst the many other complex characteristics that make us the individuals we are. In the context of crime-solving, our own unique DNA, recovered from cells left behind at a crime scene, can be invaluable as a means of identifying us as the perpetrator or otherwise. Anything from semen in a case of rape, to blood at the scene of a murder can be recovered by trained forensic officers, and analysed to identify the person who left such a telling clue behind.

Now a "Low Copy" DNA profiling technique has been developed, whereby the profile of an offender can be extracted when only a very few cells have been left behind at the scene. Such unique biological cells can be as small as a millionth of the size of a grain of salt. So an infinitesimal droplet of saliva or even a tiny speck of sweat on a surface can be subjected to the mind-boggling analysis of the Low Copy DNA technique and, if recovered properly, used to help convict an offender.

The potential for conviction via DNA can of course become considerably weakened if a number of different people have touched or handled the piece of evidence recovered, as for example may be the case with a gun that has been used in a number of murders by different perpetrators. A potential suspect's DNA can become contaminated by all the other different DNA profiles that have been deposited on the weapon – not just from previous users of that gun of course, but perhaps also from a forensic investigator who has clumsily recovered, or incorrectly handled or processed the weapon.

So I appreciate there are complexities surrounding the science of DNA profiling in cases of murder. The DNA "magic bullet" evidence isn't always easy to find. And even when such evidence is found, defence lawyers are experts at dissecting the forensic retrieval process with a view to identifying possible opportunities for the contamination or botching of the evidence.

However, in my opinion, the Ruger which was used to murder my brother and at least three other people merited scrutiny, including testing for DNA profiling. There are many murder cases, where the police don't have the luxury of having the murder weapon in their possession for testing. Therefore, having the Ruger available to them in this instance should have been invaluable to investigators in their quest for the truth. Even a micro-grain of established fact might just lead to some additional evidential opportunity.

I therefore requested that the HET carry out on the Ruger whatever DNA profiling techniques were available to them through the Northern Ireland Forensic Science Laboratory. As I expected, they initially refused. They indicated that there were concerns, since this weapon had obviously been used in several murders. They said they had to take into account the fact that there could therefore have been multiple users of the Ruger involved in those incidents. They said they could not objectively account for the handling and correct evidential storage of this gun in the time between John's murder and its recovery in 1990 in Belgium.

I didn't disagree with their interpretation of these facts, but I again suggested that they should be doing the job they were set up to do – that is, to pursue every available evidential strand in an in-depth cold case review of each and every unsolved case they had been tasked with investigating. I cited once more the obvious fact that they now had an actual murder weapon in their possession, something not always available in their difficult task of reviewing so many unsolved murders. They had a Ruger hand gun that they knew had been used to kill at least four people. Surely in their quest for the truth, I asked, the families of those who had been murdered with that gun deserved to have every possible avenue of investigation explored by the body which had been set up to help them? And was that body, the HET, not just legally but morally obliged to seek out that truth when such an avenue of investigation had presented itself?

Now the HET were in a quandary. They were obviously aware of the controversy surrounding the case of the Omagh bombing, where the validity of Low Copy DNA profiling had been questioned. During that legal process, it had been strongly argued that if the police were not able to account for every movement of an exhibit, and prove that each person who had handled it, whether in the police or among forensic personnel, had done so in controlled circumstances, then any forensic evidence obtained could be rendered useless.

I then asked them whether, on the basis of what they knew about the Ruger, they felt they should refuse my request for DNA analysis outright. And whether, on the basis of what they didn't know about the professional and correct storage, or otherwise, of this weapon over many years in Belgium, they also felt my request should be refused.

Their response was to seek independent legal advice from Queen's Counsel concerning the viability of any evidence obtained by forensic DNA examination, now many years later. Queen's Counsel considered the question carefully, and advised the HET that forensic evidence should not be automatically excluded, simply because the handling of the exhibit lacked continuity or integrity; they concluded that each case should be considered on its own merits.

After further delays, the HET finally took the decision to submit the Ruger to the Forensic Science Service of Northern Ireland, to be examined for the presence of both fingerprints and potential DNA profiling. Naturally I was pleased with this outcome, but at the same time felt annoyed that the decision to proceed had only been taken because of ongoing pressure from a victim's family member. My strong impression was that, instead of automatically doing the right thing, the HET investigators seemed more concerned with finding excuses for not doing their jobs properly.

When they finally became available, the initial results from the forensics lab showed that there were no useable fingerprints on the Ruger. So that avenue for potential identification was eliminated. The subsequent detailed DNA analysis of the weapon resulted in a low-level mixture of partial DNA – from at least two individual sources – being obtained from the area underneath the pistol grip. The results stated that the DNA mixture contained only basic information and was not suitable for meaningful comparison.

All of this meant that, although it was not possible to positively identify a single killer from the mixed profile DNA which had been obtained, it might be possible to eliminate somebody from the frame – such as perhaps a suspect, or suspects, in my brother's murder. Therefore, what they were basically saying was that, if the HET had a DNA profile for the main suspect in my brother's murder, then comparing that person's DNA with the profile they had obtained from the Ruger pistol grip might enable them to establish that that person's DNA was not present, but could not allow them to say with certainty that it was on the Ruger.

Again, frustrated with the endless dead ends and the apparent doublespeak on the part of the HET, I simply asked them if they had carried out that procedure of comparison, and therefore been able to eliminate my brother's suspected killer, or not. Yet again, I was astounded by their answer. They told me that the Police Service of Northern Ireland, and formerly the RUC, did not hold DNA samples for the two men who had been arrested in connection with John's murder in early 1989. They went on to say that the current circumstances in 2008 did not present the HET with a reason to re-arrest these two suspects in order to obtain their DNA samples for the purposes of comparison.

Call me cynical, but again, I wasn't sure if what they meant when they said "the current circumstances" was to imply that, in the new era of so-called peace, it was not deemed prudent to go rocking the fragile political boat by arresting known suspects and trying to obtain DNA samples for investigation. Was the peace process effectively offering some sort of immunity or amnesty to known suspects? Was the HET simply a sham exercise that was never aimed at finding the actual truth? If this was the case, then what was the point of having the HET in the first place? What was this HET sham really all about?

They then indicated that the two suspects could be approached by them and asked to provide DNA samples voluntarily – but that the HET had assessed, in view of the backgrounds and demeanour of these two men during previous arrest, when they refused to speak for the entire duration of the three days of their interview, that they would be unlikely to cooperate. They added that, since the samples could only confirm that the DNA of these suspects was not present on the Ruger, it would not be a viable line of enquiry anyway.

By this time I felt I was reaching the end of my tether. I asked my senior HET contact, what was the point of doing the DNA analysis on the Ruger, if they were never ever going to be able to compare any samples found on the weapon with the DNA of the IRA members they suspected of killing my brother? And when they already had made the decision anyway that they were never going to re-arrest those known suspects as part of their in-depth cold case review?

I never did get a satisfactory answer from the HET to what I consider were valid questions from a victim's brother, who just wanted to find out the truth and had been told by Government, and assured by endless Chief Constables, that the HET was set up to help provide that truth and closure. The simple fact is that, in my case and in many other cases, they didn't.

Chapter Twenty-Six

The Ruger Serial Number

Having exhausted my search for the truth using possible Low Copy DNA technology, I still had questions for the team of HET investigators, some of whom jetted in each week from various parts of the UK and jetted home again at weekends. I was determined that they should earn their inflated salaries.

I remembered the news report, which had appeared in *An Phoblacht* in March 1988 and mentioned that the "backup" Ruger Michael Stone had used in Milltown Cemetery – and which was taken from him by some of the mourners and handed over to the IRA – had had its serial number removed. So I was simply curious, considering the parallels, to know if it was possible that the Ruger used to kill John was the one that Michael Stone had used in his ambush on the funeral in Milltown Cemetery.

Throughout most of the second half of 2010, I therefore decided to focus on the official manufacturer's serial number on the Ruger – or rather its absence, since someone had taken time to remove it with a grinding tool or wheel. I asked that the HET carry out whatever process was forensically available to them to try to retrieve the ground-down serial number on this weapon.

My senior HET contact, David Brown's, first response was to ask why I wanted to know this serial number. He was curious about my need to know this, but I was more curious about his curiosity: after all, why wouldn't I want to pursue that line? More importantly, why didn't they want to find out the serial number of a murder weapon that was now finally in their possession – a weapon, which had been confirmed ballistically in contemporaneous RUC investigations as having been used to kill at least four people? And surely that serial number information could potentially help with other investigations? Was cross-referencing murders not important?

I was angry with David Brown for his off-hand response about the relevance of the serial number of the gun, and I told him in no uncertain terms how I felt. I said that it wasn't his brother who had been murdered: it was my brother. It was my mum and dad, who had died prematurely from the pain and stress caused by losing their son in this way. And therefore it bloody well did matter to me. And if it was important to me, then he should do his job and try to answer my questions. He didn't ever ask me again why it mattered.

He said that the serial number had been filed down completely, and was no longer visible, and that it was therefore no longer possible to recover it. I disagreed, however. Maybe I had watched too many CSI type programmes and documentaries. Such media analysis of crime scenes on our television screens virtually every night of the week, along with the abundance of true crime magazines and books now at our disposal, means that we've all the potential to become armchair crime scene investigators. Those 1960s and 1970s detectives we grew to love – the Columbos and the Kojaks – have been replaced by blood-splatter experts and forensic scientists in real life, courtroom docu-dramas and news footage. And of course we now also have at our fingertips the huge information resource of the Internet.

I scanned Google for more information, and then I wrote to Mr David Cox, the Head of the Historical Enquiries Team, on 24 August 2010:

Dear Mr Cox,

I am sure there have been numerous instances of weapons being used in criminal and terrorist incidents and subsequently recovered by the RUC/PSNI that were found to have had their serial numbers removed, to deliberately conceal the identity of the owner or perpetrator. Sadly, there have been many murders carried out here in Northern Ireland, for which the police do not have the luxury of a recovered weapon to help them in their investigations.

I would therefore have thought that, having a recovered Ruger in your possession, that can be confirmed as having been used in the murders of at least four people … the HET would be delighted with having such an important piece of evidence, and feel it was their duty and responsibility to use every means available to try to trace the history of the weapon that was used to kill my brother John, Colin Abernethy, Nick Spanos and Stephen Melrose. And in doing so, to potentially link that Ruger to other unsolved murders. I consider the casual dismissal of my request and the HET [response to] my genuine concerns to be totally unsatisfactory. The simple answer – that the ground-down serial number could not be revealed – was at the time both annoying and disappointing. But I also now consider it [to be] totally incorrect.

I have carried out my own research … into "Serial Number Retrieval on Weapons", and enclose copies of documents I have sourced on the Internet for your reference. Based on this information, I am surprised that a senior investigator within the HET and with the level of overall expertise that is available within the structures of the HET and its connections with the PSNI and the Forensic Science Laboratory here in Northern Ireland, and indeed with forensic laboratories worldwide, can arrive at the conclusion that a deliberately ground-down serial number cannot be revealed.

As you will see from the enclosed literature, which I really feel should not be news to you and your HET cold case review team, not only is it possible to retrieve serial numbers from weapons using long-established methods, but it would appear that, as far back as the year 2000, a new and revolutionary method was tested and adapted by the South African Police Service to successfully examine many such recovered weapons that had had their serial numbers deliberately removed by grinding or other means.

This method is easily carried out using a handheld Electromagnetic Yoke along with a Magnetic Etching Process, and produces positive results within literally minutes, instead of the usual hours other older methods required – and without compromising the structure or evidential integrity of the weapon being analysed.

The internet information I provided with my letter showed that when new guns are stamped by the manufacturer, the pressure used is so great that the serial number digits will travel through the metal and alter the structure underneath its surface. This means that removing the surface serial number will still leave the underlying metal molecules intact in the outline shape of the numbers that have been stamped on the gun. Using special scientific techniques therefore, it is possible to discern the outline of the serial number on the underlying metal. This was not just the stuff of television crime scene investigation dramas, but a real life investigative technique, and one the HET didn't seem to know about or wish to pursue. I concluded my letter as follows:

> I consider that the HET should feel it is important to establish whether the Ruger they have in their possession might be linked to other murders, by trying to reveal the serial number of that Ruger. I certainly consider it a legitimate question, which I deserve to have answered; the families of the other known victims of this murder weapon might also consider this to be the case.
>
> I therefore request that the HET organise to have the Ruger .357 Magnum in your possession examined using the recognised Scientific Serial Number Retrieval methods available, in order to reveal its serial number.
>
> I also request that the HET, having successfully retrieved the serial number, check it against any relevant manufacturer's serial number database, to establish where that serial numbered weapon was originally supplied from and despatched to. I also request that … the serial number … be checked against any relevant American manufacturer's serial number database to establish if it was supplied to the RUC.

> I look forward to hearing from you.

> George Larmour

Chapter Twenty-Seven

The Ruger Report

After yet another delay, which I knew by now to expect, the HET agreed to have the Ruger tested at the Northern Ireland Forensic Science Laboratories in Carrickfergus, County Antrim. They said they would do whatever scientific tests were available, to try and retrieve the original manufacturer's serial number.

On 15 December 2010, I received the HET report. The comprehensive document began by outlining once more the various questions that I was seeking answers to, including whether or not the Ruger .357 revolver that was used to murder John was in fact originally owned by the RUC, as well as the issue of whether it might be the same weapon used by Michael Stone during his gun and grenade attack at Milltown Cemetery on 16 March 1988.

The report went on to clarify that the HET had initially contemplated not attempting to recover the serial number of the gun, since it deemed that doing so would not lead to the identity of the gunmen. However, based on my own assertion that not all lines of inquiry had been adequately explored, they subsequently accepted that they should have the weapon analysed, and had instructed a senior scientific officer from Forensic Science Northern Ireland to do so.

The report then presented this expert's detailed outline of his findings. Although worn, the weapon was in working condition. The original hand grips had been removed and replaced with rubber versions. A lanyard ring had been added at the base of the hand grip; the process of adding the lanyard ring by drilling a hole in the base of the hand grip appeared to have obliterated the third digit and the hyphen of the factory-stamped serial number on the base of the grip.

The forensic officer confirmed that the American Ruger manufacturer stamped all such guns with an eight-digit number on the base of the grip in the format 123–45678. He went on to state that the original, factory-stamped serial number on the base had been obliterated by some sort of grinding process, involving, in his estimation, the use of a nine-inch grinding wheel. He noted that there was evidence of similar grinding on the left side of the frame, just below the cylinder. He cautioned however that this type of grinding wheel could not be matched to any particular tool, since a grinding wheel wears as it is used.

The forensic officer stated that, although there were no longer any records available, his inquiries suggested that the RUC armouries installed lanyard rings at the base and also rubberised the hand grips on all new Speed Six Rugers they received. He confirmed that this involved drilling into the frame, which resulted in the removal of part of the original serial number – usually the third digit and the hyphen.

He then explained that, in order to retain a record of the correct serial number on each weapon, the RUC armouries would have then engraved the complete serial number again on the left side of the gun's frame, below the cylinder. Based on this information, the senior forensic scientist therefore felt it was "likely" that the Ruger in question had been originally owned by the RUC. He then explained that the stamping of serial numbers into steel does change its structure, in this instance making that particular portion of the weapon harder or more resistant than the surrounding, unstamped steel. Therefore, when that area is etched using acids, the metal will be removed at different rates, meaning that stamped numbers and letters might become visible for a short time during the process.

He confirmed that he had attempted, using a process known as chemical etching, to recover the serial number on the Ruger. He had thereby managed to reveal the number "6" in fifth position and the number "9" in sixth position, i.e.: XXX–X69XX. He was already aware that the Ruger manufacturer stamped their Speed Six revolvers with numbers beginning with either "15" or "16", and therefore his tests so far suggested the serial number comprised either 15X-X69XX or 16X-X69XX.

He then said that, because the serial number on the side of the gun had been engraved, rather than stamped, he had used a polishing technique rather than an etching process to try to reveal that serial number. The only number which had become visible during that process appeared to be a "9" in the seventh position; some additional work revealed a partial number in the eighth position, which appeared to be the top of a number "2". His tentative conclusion was therefore that the original serial number of the Ruger could be 15X–X6992 or 16X–X6992, although this was by no means a definite conclusion.

After presenting this officer's specific findings, the report went on to confirm that between March 1979 and August 1986, the RUC took delivery of 7,346 Speed Six Ruger Magnum .357 revolvers, for issue to their staff. However it was stated that records, relating to when or to whom these Rugers were allocated, no longer existed.

Apparently in the following years, over 40 of these RUC Rugers had been somehow lost or stolen. The HET had checked with the PSNI in 2008 and had been informed that there were only records for 13 of these guns that had never been recovered, and that none of the serial numbers on file for the 13 weapons in question matched the partial number revealed on the gun by the scientific officer. It is disturbing to think that there are still 13 RUC Rugers unaccounted for out there somewhere.

The report then confirmed what I already knew: that the Ruger .357 Magnum had been used on two other occasions apart from for the murder of my brother John in October 1988. On 9 September 1988, Colin Abernethy was shot and killed with the Ruger; and on 27 May 1990, it was used again in the murder of two Australian tourists in Holland – Stephen Melrose and Nick Spanos.

Concerning the murders carried out by Michael Stone at Milltown Cemetery in March 1988, three spent cartridges from a Ruger .357 revolver had been recovered at the scene. However, despite the HET carrying out extensive searches, it seemed that these three cartridges no longer existed – meaning that there was no opportunity to compare them with any test fire results from the weapon used to kill John.

In conclusion, it was stated that the gun used to kill John was "likely" to have been one of the Rugers originally owned by the RUC; unfortunately however, no records existed to show who the gun might have been issued to. The report also deduced that it was "possible" that the gun under investigation was the one used by Michael Stone at Milltown Cemetery, but that there was no direct evidence to support this claim. However, the report confirmed that there was no doubt that the Ruger was in the hands of the Provisional IRA by September 1988, and that it was one of their members who used it to murder John.

Finally, the report acknowledged my request to view the weapon personally and stated that arrangements for me to do so were currently being put in place.

Chapter Twenty-Eight

Drawing My Own Conclusions

After resolutely refusing to go away and persisting in asking the Historical Enquiries Team endless questions, I felt I was at last getting somewhere in my quest for the truth. Yet even now, their use of politically correct, academic, civil-service type language was irksome in the extreme.

Dotted throughout this latest report, as with every previous one in the three years I had been dealing with them, were words and expressions such as "likely", "our enquiries suggest", and "it is possible", carefully dropped into paragraphs in just the right places to ensure that all possible interpretations would be catered for. But I had learned a long time ago that the HET rarely said things directly, and so I shouldn't have been surprised to find all these caveats that cleverly covered their backs.

Was the Ruger that was used to kill my brother John originally owned by the RUC? Was it the same weapon that was used by Michael Stone in Milltown Cemetery? Two simple straightforward questions that I had asked the HET to answer, as part of their supposed in-depth cold case review of my brother's murder. In the absence of any clear, definitive replies on their part, I realised that I would have to draw conclusions of my own.

I read the report a number of times and satisfied myself that my brother John, an RUC officer with 12 years' service, had been murdered on 11 October 1988 by the IRA with a Speed Six Ruger Magnum .357 revolver that was originally owned by the RUC. Despite the cautious, non-committal language of the HET, I felt, on reading the detail, that there was no other interpretation possible. All the evidence was there. The RUC ordered and issued Speed Six Ruger Magnum .357 revolvers to their staff. These weapons allowed officers to reload quickly, using special Speed Clips containing six bullets. Before issuing a new Ruger to each serving officer, the RUC armouries had routinely replaced the original Ruger manufacturer's smooth hand grips with special rubber grips on each weapon. They had then drilled a hole in the base of the pistol hand grip of each revolver to insert a lanyard ring, so that the weapons could be secured to a waist belt, thereby avoiding a scenario where the gun would be snatched from an officer's holster.

By drilling this lanyard ring hole in the base of the pistol hand grip, the RUC had unfortunately drilled through the third digit and hyphen of the original manufacturer's stamped serial number. To facilitate future identification, the RUC armouries had therefore engraved the full manufacturer's serial number again on the left side of each weapon just below the cylinder, something the manufacturer never did.

The Speed Six Ruger .357 revolver currently stored in the Forensic Science Laboratory of Northern Ireland, which was used to murder my brother, has all these features. So, despite a reluctance to commit themselves to a definitive "yes" on paper, it is not just "likely" that this weapon was originally owned by the RUC, as stated in the HET report. It undoubtedly is an original RUC-issue Ruger.

I found it curious that records no longer existed of the serial numbers of the 7,346 Speed Six Ruger revolvers the RUC took delivery of and issued to their staff between March 1979 and August 1986. In order to ensure future identification, the RUC's official armouries had undertaken the painstaking process of engraving the full serial number a second time on each weapon on the left of the frame just below the cylinder. And yet the HET report was stating that the RUC did not then keep a record of all those serial numbers.

However, further investigations on my part revealed that there had in fact been files of the Ruger serial numbers. My source confirmed to me that these records had been collated and stored in a location within Northern Ireland, but that at a certain point, it had been discovered that the building they were stored in had been insulated with asbestos sheeting. It was suggested to me that some of the asbestos cladding had subsequently been disturbed, and that the files had been contaminated with asbestos dust. Yet, instead of carefully retrieving the files under strict asbestos handling guidelines, and copying them, someone had decided that it was more appropriate to completely destroy these carefully collated records. Was the asbestos story true – or was it concocted to ensure that no one could access the serial numbers?

I questioned my senior contact within the Historical Enquiries Team, as to why they had even bothered asking the Forensic Science Laboratory of Northern Ireland to try to retrieve the ground down serial number on the Ruger? Surely a simple request to the PSNI HQ would have shown that this exercise was utterly pointless, considering that there was never the slightest chance of matching any such recovered serial number to any of the RUC Rugers that were ordered from America? It was like the pointless exercise with the DNA testing on the Ruger that I had previously requested. I felt that the HET were just going through the motions of obliging me, and that they were therefore simply patronising me, without any meaningful expectation of worthwhile conclusions being arrived at.

My second question had been equally straightforward. Was the Ruger the gun used by Michael Stone in the attack on Milltown Cemetery in 1988? Again, the HET report provides just enough information to hint at a positive answer, but still manages to create ongoing frustration and confusion.

I accept of course that it might be difficult, if not impossible, for the HET to trace every scrap of physical evidence pertaining to every single murder case they have been tasked to re-investigate. There must be thousands of pieces of stored evidence, from tyre track and footprint moulds taken from crime scenes, to items of clothing or personal items accidentally discarded by fleeing killers, to fingerprints, blood samples, and scenes-of-crime photographs, to bullet fragments, cartridges and actual weapons.

So they couldn't find the three Milltown Cemetery .357 revolver cartridges that might hold the key to confirming that the Ruger they have in their possession was the one used by Michael Stone that day. A cynical person might conclude that it seems very convenient that these three important pieces of evidence appear to have been misplaced, carelessly handled and not properly stored away for future evidential purposes. Did someone in the RUC not want those three Ruger cartridges to be kept as evidence? Did someone consider it would stir up potential accusations of collusion and damaging PR for the RUC, if it could be confirmed that Michael Stone had access to a police-issue weapon?

But, having accepted at face value that these cartridges are indeed no longer traceable, are the HET also suggesting that RUC detectives and forensics specialists didn't examine and compare Ruger bullet fragments recovered when Colin Abernethy was murdered on the train at Finaghy on 9 September 1988, against the Ruger bullet taken from John Murray who was, as stated publicly by Michael Stone, killed with his Ruger in Milltown Cemetery? Are they also suggesting that detectives and forensic specialists didn't examine and compare the Ruger bullet fragments recovered in Barnam's World of Ice Cream with the Ruger bullet fired by Michael Stone that killed John Murray? And are they suggesting that again, no forensics were ever requested for analysis by RUC detectives back in 1992, to enable comparison between the Ruger bullet fragments recovered in Roermond, Holland after the murders of Stephen Melrose and Nick Spanos, and the bullet that killed John Murray in Milltown Cemetery?

Michael Stone has publicly stated that he shot and killed John Murray with the Ruger he was carrying that day. In the book, *None Shall Divide Us* (Blake Publishing, 1992), he describes what happened when he was confronted by John Murray. Michael Stone said that a brick bounced off his head and that he suddenly noticed a young man on his own, full of rage, who seemed to appear out of nowhere. He said this young man was shouting, "Come on, you Orange bastard," and yelling back to others, "Over here, he's over here, and he's out of ammo."

He said that he then took his Ruger out of his coat but at that stage had not intended to use it. He declared that he told the young man to "F**k off right now, just go", and pointed the Ruger at him. But that the young man, despite seeing the gun, stood his ground and continued to throw bricks at Stone.

He then relates that this young man suddenly moved forward and challenged him. Stone said that he fired one shot, which hit the young man in the neck and that the bullet must have travelled down into his body, as he died instantly. Stone said he subsequently found out that his pursuer was named John 'Minto' Murray and that he regretted shooting him that day.

After reading their report, I discussed my concerns with the HET at length in face-to-face meetings. I did not get any satisfactory answers. There appeared to be no desire to deal with my questions about the Ruger used by Michael Stone and its possible connection with the murders of my brother and Colin Abernethy, Stephen Melrose and Nick Spanos. I find it strange that the RUC and the HET could easily confirm that the murders of my brother John and Colin Abernethy and Stephen Melrose and Nick Spanos are all connected to the disputed Ruger – these facts are there in black and white in the correspondence from the HET. Yet they cannot or will not give me a straight answer as to whether or not it is the same Ruger that was used by Michael Stone in Milltown Cemetery.

I suggested that the HET take the Ruger to Michael Stone, and ask him if he would be willing to identify it as being the one he used. Failing this, I asked them if they would provide me with photographs of the Ruger, so that I might take these to Michael Stone myself, to see if he would be able and willing to confirm if it had belonged to him. Stone once said that he adored the Ruger he used in his failed attempt to murder Sinn Féin Councillor John Joe Davey in February 1988; the same one he would use in Milltown Cemetery weeks later. So I thought he might be aware of some particular markings on this weapon and perhaps be willing to identify them, and in doing so, answer my simple question in my search for the truth. The HET refused to give me photographs of the Ruger and they also refused to take it to Michael Stone for identification.

The more the HET tried to avoid doing their job, the more I was determined to demand they did it properly. From what I had read, I believed it was the same Ruger. I couldn't understand why they found what I was asking so difficult. All I wanted, and all I still want, is the truth, every bit of the truth associated with the murder of my brother.

Chapter Twenty-Nine

Ronald Reagan's Rugers

Ronald Wilson Reagan, former Hollywood actor and Governor of California, was the 40th President of the United States of America. His Irish roots reached back to a tiny rural farming town, Ballyporeen in County Tipperary. His great-grandfather, Michael Regan (who later changed his name), emigrated to the United States of America in the 1860s. From those humble family beginnings, great-grandson Ronald entered the Oval Office on 20 January 1981, and his presidency ended on 20 January 1989. He left office just a few months after my brother John was murdered in Barnam's, a small American-style ice cream parlour situated almost 3,500 miles away from that iconic Presidential White House.

During his two terms in office, President Reagan of course made many decisions. I'm sure a number of these were his own, and based on his personal opinions and beliefs. However others no doubt were really made by his administration staff, and simply countersigned by him with his official seal. Little did I realise that one such decision, associated with the Reagan administration during that period, would surface during my own investigations into my brother's murder.

My searches indicate that, during Ronald Reagan's term in office, his administration and therefore, by implication he, the President, became involved in the Royal Ulster Constabulary's decision to equip its serving police officers in Northern Ireland with new, more modern weapons.

The RUC's new weapon of choice was the Speed Six Ruger .357 Magnum revolver. It was sturdy and powerful but also lightweight and reliable. An additional facility, which allowed special speed clips of six bullets to be loaded simultaneously, was another compelling factor in favour of the Speed Six Ruger for the arming of RUC officers, who were under daily threat from the IRA, now equipped themselves with ever more sophisticated and powerful new weapons. The RUC needed the new guns to help them compete, and had decided to place an order for over 7,000 units with the Ruger manufacturer in America.

This was at a time when relations and cooperation between the American and British governments were good. The media on both sides of the Atlantic commented on the "special relationship" that had been created between Prime Minister Margaret Thatcher and President Reagan. Among other things, the quality of this relationship was to be crucial to the creation of the Anglo-Irish Agreement.

However, in terms of British–American relations, matters relating to the "Irish question" were always delicate. Both governments were keen to ensure that nothing would tip the balance in their search for a lasting solution to the problems of Northern Ireland, but each also had their own separate interests to keep in mind. The American administration's desire to cooperate with the British Government was tempered by the necessity to keep a careful focus on the reaction of the Irish-American lobby in the US. Many Irish Americans were voicing their concerns about the Troubles back in their ancestral home of Northern Ireland. They protested about the deaths of Irish citizens at the hands of the British army and RUC on the streets of Belfast and Derry. They made little or no distinction between the legal police force and the loyalist death squads of illegal paramilitary groups.

Many were vociferous supporters of the IRA's right to resist British rule, and the right of Irish citizens to arm themselves to oppose this "occupation" of the North. A fundraising organisation based in the USA, the Irish Northern Aid Committee – more commonly known as NORAID – was set up soon after the Troubles started in 1969. It was supposedly a financial support group for the broader republican movement, but there were allegations that NORAID gave direct assistance to the Provisional Irish Republican Army (PIRA). This was consistently denied by NORAID, but despite these repeated denials, in 1977 the American government obliged NORAID to officially register as an agent of PIRA. NORAID continued with their sustained vocal support for Irish republicans during Ronald Reagan's years in office.

Against this backdrop, someone within the Reagan administration decided that it wouldn't look good politically for a US government with an Irish-American President to be seen to be supplying new weapons for the arming of the RUC. No doubt those with a finger on the Irish-American pulse felt that the Reagan administration couldn't be seen to approve the sale of weapons which could ultimately be used by officers of the RUC to shoot, and perhaps kill, Irish citizens, even as part of legitimate crime-fighting duties.

The conclusions of my own private investigations, which were confirmed in documents released to the local media in January 2012 under the UK's 30-year declassification rule, indicated that the US Congressional ban against selling weapons to the RUC, enacted by Congress in 1979 following pressure by organised groups in the Irish-American community, was being broken. The 30-year declassified documents do not specify if the White House was aware that the ban was being broken, or if in fact the weapons were surreptitiously smuggled by the British Government without Washington's knowledge. However, one of the newspaper journalists who had access to the declassified documents in 2012, stated that he had testimony from a former RUC officer to the effect that the Reagan administration had been aware of the shipments, and had simply turned a blind eye to what was being done. So was a deal concocted between the Reagan administration and Margaret Thatcher's government, to bypass the Congressional ban on supplying weapons directly to the RUC? An arrangement which saw the 7,346 new Speed Six Rugers, ordered by the RUC in Northern Ireland, being shipped instead to the Metropolitan Police in London, who then despatched the new weapons to RUC Headquarters in Belfast in batches of 500 and over a period of time, thereby avoiding the impression that the weapons had been supplied in bulk from America to the RUC?

My perception is that, from America's standpoint, it was, politically, okay for English police officers to shoot and kill English criminals or terrorists; it was also, in fact, okay for the RUC to use the new Rugers to maim and kill Irish citizens in Belfast and Derry, as part of their day-to-day fight against crime and terrorism – just as long as the Reagan administration couldn't be seen to be supplying these new weapons to them directly. As Geronimo in my schoolboy ambush days would have said: "White man speak with forked tongue." Wise words.

Because of this "special arrangement", and the haphazard nature of the arrival in Belfast of so many different batches of weapons, the new Rugers were quickly delivered to different policing divisions soon after they arrived in Northern Ireland. As we know, the RUC armouries did take the time to fit new pistol grips to each weapon, a lanyard ring and to have the serial numbers duplicated on the side of each weapon for identification purposes. But significantly, possibly because of time constraints caused by the drip-feed, small batch delivery arrangement between America, London and Belfast, and then to the different RUC divisions throughout Northern

Ireland, it seems that one vital procedure was often overlooked. Each gun should have been test-fired and its ballistic details recorded. It seems that this was done for some of the new Rugers, but not for all.

During manufacture, each individual gun barrel ends up with distinctive rotating grooves inside it. Therefore, every barrel contains its own unique grooves, which, as distinguishing features, are essentially the equivalent of fingerprints. When a weapon is fired, the grooves inside the barrel leave their mirror image imprints on the bullet as it travels along the inside of the barrel. So, in order to establish whether a specific weapon has been used in a murder, for example, a forensic scientist can match the grooves left on a bullet recovered at the scene of a crime with grooves on a test bullet fired from the same weapon.

Had a comprehensive ballistics test-fire procedure been carried out for each weapon in the consignment of Rugers supplied to the RUC and the results securely stored for future reference, there would have been a record of the "fingerprint" of each of these guns, meaning that my original question to the HET – about whether the Ruger used to kill John was an RUC weapon – could have been easily answered. All investigators would have had to do would have been to test-fire the Ruger now in HET possession and crossmatch it with the official bulk database of results for all the new Rugers supplied in that US order. Such a simple exercise would have avoided the long and laborious serial number retrieval process, and easily confirmed what I believed – that the Ruger was indeed one of the 7,346 Margaret Thatcher/ Ronald Reagan "special relationship" weapons ordered by the RUC in 1979.

Chapter Thirty

A Close Encounter

I t was Thursday, 20 January 2011, and I was sitting in the bitterly cold reception area of the Northern Ireland Forensic Science Laboratory in Carrickfergus, County Antrim.

A white Christmas had outlived its welcome. The novelty had worn off, and a prolonged spell of freezing snow had begun to annoy more than please those of us who had to live with it. The paper-thin portakabin reception hut wasn't designed for a harsh January. As I sat in one of the two rigid plastic chairs provided, I suspected that they didn't expect or encourage ordinary visitors here. Was it really so cold, or was thinking about the purpose of my visit making me shiver? I rubbed my arms to try to add some warmth to my chilled memories.

The Historical Enquiries Team had always known I was a nuisance. But even I was surprised they had actually agreed to my demand to see and inspect the Ruger which had been used to kill my brother. Perhaps their own cold exterior had thawed, as we all wished the snow would, and they had been touched by some of the lingering compassionate spirit of the season.

With my gloved hands deeply stuffed into my overcoat pockets for extra heat, I waited for the senior firearms specialist to come and escort me to where the Ruger was securely stored. This was the same man who had carried out the DNA profiling search and serial number retrieval processes I had originally requested. I wasn't sure what emotions would surface when I saw the weapon which had killed John.

The man in question arrived, and signed me in. Although younger than me, he somehow reminded me of my school chemistry teacher. He was friendly and chatty, as we hurried through the grounds of the vast complex. He led me along a labyrinth of corridors and past numerous keypad security protected doors, to his office – a cramped space with a small desk covered in files.

As the senior forensic officer rummaged through his desk drawer for something, I noticed that the wall to his left was covered with a large poster, like one of those World Cup football team posters you might see on any child's bedroom wall. This one however had detailed drawings of dozens of handguns and rifles. The wall facing his desk was covered in newspaper cuttings, most with headlines referring to shooting incidents. Were these reminders of past successes he had investigated, or goals yet to be scored?

We left his office and again made our way through yet more key-coded security doors, into a room with white laboratory coats hanging on pegs and a basket of those blue plastic bags that you see forensics officers on television wearing over their shoes. My companion donned one of the white lab coats himself and politely asked me if I would remove my coat and gloves, and put on one as well. Apart from me now looking like a fully qualified forensics officer, I couldn't help thinking that this seemed a bit of a pointless exercise, considering all the evidential integrity of the weapon had already been compromised anyway.

We then passed through one final security door into the central hub of this Forensic Science establishment. It looked nothing like the usual backdrop on CSI type television dramas. There was no large team of scientists, busily dissecting minute specimens or inspecting slides under rows of microscopes for clues; no detectives standing waiting for conclusive DNA results to be handed over by the forensics team, before racing off to arrest and charge another culprit. This was a quiet, brightly lit, standard laboratory similar to the one I had worked in at Gallaher's tobacco factory in Belfast, in my first job after leaving school. This was pristine but soulless – just what you would expect in an evidence-analysing environment. There were no other exhibits on any of the benches. Perhaps they had removed unrelated evidence from my inquisitive gaze, or maybe a rare visit by a victim's bothersome brother required an extra tidy-up that day.

There were two other people in the room, a man and a woman, neither of whom were wearing lab coats. They were introduced to me as members of the Historical Enquiries Team who had been asked to attend. I had never met them before. They were polite and professional, but I sensed they were less than happy at having to be there to facilitate my viewing of the Ruger.

I had already been instructed by David Brown, my senior HET contact, that it was with reluctance that they were allowing me to inspect the gun at close quarters, and that there were strict conditions. I was not permitted to touch it. In fact, I was told that if I did, I could be arrested.

I have to admit that a devilish little voice in my head was inviting me to do just that, as I was ushered across the laboratory to a cardboard box that sat on the middle of the central bench. I was already mentally imagining the editor's front page headline for the first editions of the *Belfast Telegraph* later that day: "Brother of Murdered Police Officer Arrested in Possession of Murder Weapon".

Would they really arrest me? Should I touch the Ruger just for the hell of it? At least it would mean that the HET had arrested someone as part of their cold case review into John's murder. That would be a first, if nothing else. The two HET staff eyed me carefully. I decided however not to annoy the forensics officer, who seemed genuinely willing to help.

He opened the cardboard box, and there it was. The Speed Six Ruger .357 Magnum revolver that had been used to kill John and at least three other people. As I stared at it, I was disturbed by a memory. The instant recollection came out of nowhere and I found it hard to hold back tears. The dark, smoky-blue colour of the metal was exactly the same as that of the shotgun I had bought many years earlier with my best friend, Sam. I could hear the screams of the hare again. That was the vivid memory that haunted my thoughts in that instant, as I looked at the Ruger, and as the forensics officer lifted it out of the evidence box and held it in the palm of his hand, close to my face.

As he started to explain the processes that had been carried out on the weapon, his voice seemed to be coming from somewhere in the distance. He could see that I wasn't focused on what he was saying, and asked if I was okay. When I nodded, he started explaining what had been done to modify the Ruger by the RUC armoury. This specialist had no qualms about talking about it as an RUC weapon. He didn't use words such as "likely" or "possibly" in his descriptions. His honesty was refreshing.

As he showed me the areas where the serial numbers had been ground off, I was surprised to see how perfect they were. I thought they would look rough and ragged, but they weren't. It looked as if the person doing it had polished the metal, patiently and with loving care, until it was smooth. I saw an impression of sticky tape left on the pistol grip. Was this perhaps where someone had taped a replacement bullet clip for quick reloading?

The man explained the procedures he had performed to search for fingerprints and extract the mixed DNA sample under the pistol grip, and how he had gone about attempting to reveal the hidden serial numbers, each time turning the Ruger over and moving it from one hand to the other. I noticed how he deliberately avoided holding it as you would when using it to shoot someone.

The gun looked smaller than I expected, but it seemed perfect for concealing in a coat pocket, and ideal for someone planning an ambush. The forensics officer asked if I had any questions, but there was nothing I could think of. It occurred to me later that he hadn't worn protective gloves when handling the gun. Maybe he knew there was no evidence worth cross-contaminating anymore.

I don't know what I expected to achieve by seeing the Ruger. Did I think there would be some eureka moment that would make sense of John's killing; that I would detect some telltale mark on it that would solve his or someone else's murder? Had I imagined I would spot something the forensics guys had missed; something that would expose unknown assassins? Had I expected to see notches carved by the different executioners, glorifying their achievements?

My visit was over too quickly and I drove home in a daze of uncertainties and with a disturbing personal memory that had long been hidden away. I wondered how many terrified screams the Ruger had managed to generate in its lifetime. I pondered once more how anyone could kill another human being – and how some thought nothing of doing it, again and again.

Chapter Thirty-One

"I was never in the IRA"

In August 2010 I was reading through a local newspaper, when I came across a story about an Australian television crew which had come to Belfast and was filming at Parliament Buildings, Stormont. After requesting an official interview with Gerry Adams, President of Sinn Féin and deputy First Minister Martin McGuinness, and being refused, they had turned up unannounced at an outdoor event there and confronted Mr Adams about his alleged involvement, membership and former leadership of the IRA.

The newspaper article explained that award-winning Australian journalist, Ross Coulthart, was investigating the 1990 murders of Stephen Melrose and Nick Spanos in Holland by the IRA. He wanted to know what role, if any, Gerry Adams had played in the sanctioning of these murders. He suggested that Adams, despite his many denials of ever having been in the organisation, was considered by many members of the public and security services to have been a member of the IRA's ruling Army Council in 1990. The article concluded by saying that, predictably, Gerry Adams had told Ross Coulthart that he had never been a member of the IRA and said that he, Mr Coulthart, "should not be coming here and presuming to make assertions and allegations like that".

When I read the article, I instantly recognised the names, Stephen Melrose and Nick Spanos. I was aware they were two Australian nationals in their 20s who had been working in the city of London as lawyers. In May 1990, accompanied by Nick's girlfriend, Vicky and Stephen's Australian wife of just nine months, Lyndal, the two young men were on a brief four-day holiday to the Netherlands, having driven over to Amsterdam from London to see the sights and visit the Van Gogh Museum.

As they had travelled back through Holland to Calais, where they were planning to take the ferry home, the four stopped off on the evening of Sunday, 27 May in Roermond, a town steeped in history near the border between Germany and the Netherlands. They enjoyed a meal in a Chinese restaurant, before leaving at around 11.00 pm to make their way back to their car, parked in the main square.

As they walked across the old cobbled square, they noticed a church with a very high steeple and illuminated clock, which stood out in the night sky. It looked majestic and beautiful in the moonlight. Stephen said he wanted to take some photos of it and other buildings around the square before they left. As it was cold, the two girls and Nick decided to get into the car while Stephen opened the hatchback door of the boot to get his camera equipment.

They didn't know that members of an IRA active service unit were watching them, and preparing to add their own piece of history to Roermond. As Stephen began taking the photographs, a Mazda car, stolen earlier that day, raced into the square and stopped abruptly a short distance away from him. Two gunmen wearing balaclavas jumped out of this vehicle and ran towards Stephen, one firing an AK-47 assault rifle, shattering the reverential silence of the peaceful square under the clock tower.

Stephen didn't stand a chance. He fell as the powerful bullets hit him. As he lay helpless on the ground and most likely already dead, the second gunman took aim with his Ruger Magnum handgun and shot the young Australian again at close range. This ruthless assassin then calmly and purposefully walked round to the side of the car, where the rest of the party were looking on in horror, and shot Nick several times as he sat, stunned, inside the vehicle.

Miraculously, both women were unhurt. As the killers were driven off into the darkness by a third member of the IRA team, the beautiful old square in Roermond was silent once again. Nick and Stephen lay dead, their lifeblood splattered on the cobbled ground beneath them. Lyndal and Vicky, their clothes stained with the blood of those they loved, stared at the scene before them in uncomprehending, shocked silence.

The ensuing media coverage in Holland and further afield reflected the general disbelief and outrage at the murders. Why would someone want to kill two innocent Australian tourists in Roermond?

Many people – including Nick and Stephen – were unaware of the dark history of the region they had been visiting that weekend. The two young men hadn't considered that their short hair and tall, strong, clean-shaven appearance, as well as their English-registered car would make them stand out as potential targets for the Provisional IRA. They weren't aware that the

IRA had sent active service units to the area to seek out and target British military personnel.

In previous attacks two years earlier, on 1 May 1988, the IRA had killed three off-duty British Royal Air Force Regiment members and wounded three others. In the first of two attacks on the same date, their active service unit opened fire on a car at the market in Roermond. The RAF members had been stationed about 20 miles away across the border in West Germany, at RAF Wildenrath.

The three airmen in the vehicle had visited bars in the area that night. It was well known that these were favourite nightspots for off-duty British service personnel. Probably deciding to have a rest before driving back to their base after an enjoyable night out, the three of them had been sleeping in their car. Just after 1.00 am and without any warning, IRA gunmen fired around 20 shots into the car with a machine-gun. Senior Aircraftman, 20-year-old Ian Shinner, originally from Cheshire in England, was killed, while his two colleagues were injured.

In a second attack about 20 minutes later, two other RAF members died in a bomb explosion in Nieuw-Bergen, about 30 miles from Roermond. They were Senior Aircraftmen John Reid and John Baxter, both originally from Glasgow in Scotland. They and a third colleague had been at a local disco and were about to drive back to the base. As the third airman opened the car door to join his friends, the vehicle exploded in a fireball. It is thought that the same IRA team had planted the car bomb earlier that evening, before travelling on to carry out the shooting in Roermond.

On 26 October the following year, 1989, an active service unit of the IRA killed another member of the Royal Air Force at Wildenrath, West Germany. He was 34-year-old Corporal Maheshkumar Islania. Known to his fellow RAF members simply as "Mick", he was driving back home with his wife and six-month-old baby daughter, Nivruti Mahesh. Having stopped at a snack bar attached to a petrol station, Mick was about to drive off, when two men approached the vehicle and opened fire with automatic weapons. One was the AK-47 assault rifle which would be used the following year in the killing of Stephen Melrose and Nick Spanos in Roermond.

Mick's out-of-control car crossed the road and mounted the opposite pavement. The gunmen chased after the car, repeatedly firing at it and into it. Mick Islania was hit a number of times and died. Amazingly his wife Smita was uninjured, but their tiny baby daughter also died in that horrific attack, from a single bullet wound to her head. Eye witnesses at the scene told of how a distraught Mrs Islania would not leave her dead baby daughter, insisting on cradling her in her arms and refusing to let her be taken from her.

In a follow-up statement, the IRA said they "profoundly regretted" the death of the baby girl, declaring that those who carried out the attack could not have known the baby was in the vehicle.

So it is clear that the IRA were already aware that the many bars and clubs and restaurants in those areas of Holland and Germany were favourite haunts of off-duty soldiers and airmen stationed in the vicinity. It wasn't difficult for them to find easy targets for their terrorist attacks, and, in their hate-clouded vision, Stephen Melrose and Nick Spanos fitted the profile of those they were looking to target.

When the tragic truth quickly emerged, the IRA was forced to acknowledge their mistake at a press conference in London, with Gerry Adams issuing a statement on their behalf, saying they "deeply regretted the tragedy". However, that declaration by the Sinn Féin President didn't stop the killings. A few weeks later, on 1 June 1990, off-duty British Army Major, Michael Dillon-Lee was murdered in front of his wife outside his home in Dortmund, West Germany. Again, the IRA assassination team used a powerful AK-47 assault rifle.

Later that day, suspected members of those two active service units of the IRA were captured and arrested in Germany and Belgium. These included Donna Maguire, Gerard Harte, Sean Hick and Paul Hughes. Guns that they had allegedly concealed in Germany and in a forest in Belgium were also recovered, among them, the Ruger and the Browning that were used previously in the attack on Barnam's in 1988. After a protracted legal battle and epic courtroom drama, all four IRA suspects were subsequently released and returned to Ireland.

Chapter Thirty-Two

Channel 7 Australia

Having read the article about Ross Coulthart and his team being in Northern Ireland, I decided to email the Channel 7 television company in Sydney, suggesting I might have information that could help their film crew in Belfast. I was quickly contacted by one of their producers, Mick, and received a further email from Ross Coulthart. Both were keen to know what information I had that could help them with their current investigation into the murders of Nick Spanos and Stephen Melrose.

After supplying them with the background to my brother's murder, I told Mick and Ross that the weapons used in the attack in Barnam's in 1988 were also connected to the murders of the two Australians in Holland in 1990. The Ruger recovered in Belgium was the specific weapon used to kill John, Stephen and Nick; and the Browning used in Barnam's was the gun that was recovered in Germany in 1990. As a top investigative journalist, Ross was naturally unwilling to accept this information without being able to verify what I was saying. I indicated that I would be willing to meet with him in Belfast at a location of his choosing, where I would be able to furnish him with the proof he required.

A few days later I met Ross for breakfast in the Fitzwilliam Hotel in Belfast. I provided him with authenticated proof about the history of the two guns, including documents provided to me by the Historical Enquiries Team. I also gave him details of additional murders connected to the two weapons and the name of the original owner of the Browning 9 mm – Corporal Derek Wood – and outlined my hypothesis about the history of the Ruger and its RUC origins.

Ross confirmed that, as part of the planned documentary, he and the crew had already travelled to Holland, Belgium and Germany, accompanied by Stephen Melrose's elderly parents, Roy and Beverley, his sisters Helen Jackson and Suzi Fraser, and Suzi's husband Ian. He said they had been able to film everything they wanted in those European locations, including an emotional

TIMELINE – COUNT DOWN TO MURDER

6 March 1988 – IRA members Sean Savage, Mairéad Farrell and Daniel McCann are killed in Gibraltar by members of the SAS. These deaths set in motion a series of murders that would also see my brother John killed, six months later, by members of the West Belfast Brigade of the IRA in revenge. Others would also die in the months ahead.

16 March 1988 – Michael Stone launches an attack inside Milltown Cemetery at the funerals of the Gibraltar Three. One of the weapons he used during the attack was a Speed Six Ruger .357 pistol. John Murray, Thomas McErlean and Kevin Brady are killed during the attack. I believe this is the same Ruger that was used by the IRA to murder my brother John six months later.

19 March 1988 – Army Corporals Derek Wood and David Howes are murdered on the day of IRA member, Kevin Brady's funeral in West Belfast. Corporal Wood's Browning 9 mm gun was taken from him and used to kill both him and Corporal Howes.

2 August 1988 – Derek Wood's Browning 9 mm is used in the murder of UDR Lance Corporal Roy Butler.

9 September 1988 – The Ruger .357 is used in the murder of Colin Abernethy on a train at Finaghy.

11 October 1988 – My brother John is murdered in Barnam's World of Ice Cream. The weapons used are Derek Wood's Browning 9 mm and a Speed Six Ruger .357 Magnum, which I believe is the one used by Michael Stone in Milltown Cemetery on 16 March 1988.

12 February 1989 – Lawyer Patrick Finucane is murdered by UDA/UFF in his home in front of his family.

26 February 1989 – Local West Belfast Estate Agent, Joseph Fenton, is murdered by the IRA after he was abducted, interrogated and admitted being an informer working for the RUC.

27 May 1990 – The Ruger .357 is used in the murder of Stephen Melrose and Nick Spanos in Holland. The two completely innocent Australian tourists were mistaken for off duty soldiers by the IRA.

2 June 1990 – The Browning 9 mm is recovered in Germany and the Speed Six Ruger .357 in Belgium.

MARCH 1988

GIBRALTAR THREE – 6 MARCH 1988

(Photographs courtesy Pacemaker Press)

In March 1988 three IRA members, *(l–r)* Sean Savage, Mairéad Farrell and Daniel McCann, were killed by the SAS in Gibraltar.

The deaths of the "Gibraltar Three", as they became known, set in motion a sequence of events that March that saw mourners attacked and killed by Michael Stone during their funerals and the subsequent murders of Corporals Derek Wood and David Howes.

Police and HET sources informed me that my brother John, unconnected to the deaths of the Gibraltar Three, was simply murdered six months later by members of the West Belfast IRA in an act of revenge and in honour of their three comrades killed in Gibraltar.

MILLTOWN CEMETERY – 16 MARCH 1988

Michael Stone used a special Speed Six Ruger .357 Magnum pistol during his attack in Milltown Cemetery. The Ruger was taken from him when he was caught by some of the mourners who pursued him. It found its way into the hands of the IRA in West Belfast.

I believe it is the same Ruger that the IRA then used to kill my brother John in Barnam's that October.

(Pacemaker Press)

CORPORALS KILLINGS – 19 MARCH 1988

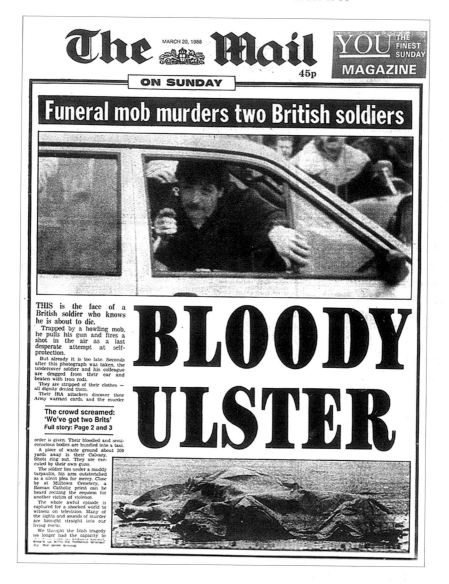

The front pages carried the iconic photograph of Corporal Derek Wood holding his Army-issue Browning 9 mm handgun. Not visible in the photograph, but beside Derek in the passenger seat, is his colleague Corporal David Howes.

Corporal Wood's 9 mm Browning was taken from him that day and used to kill both him and Corporal Howes. It was subsequently used six months later by the IRA at the murder of my brother John in Barnam's.

World of Ice Cream

When you enter the new
Barnam's Ice Cream Parlour
you're entering a world of
exotic flavours.

Ice Cream and Sorbets freshly
made with natural fruit.

*Tantalise your taste buds with
flavours like.......*

*Strawberry & Quantro,
Forest Berris, Passion
Fruit, Chocolate Ripple,
Irish Coffee, Peach, Tutti
Frutti, English Toffee,
Champagne, Mango,
Mandarin and lots
more....*

**587 Lisburn Road,
Belfast
NOW OPEN!**

Barnam's opened for business in July 1988.

We simply wanted Barnam's to be a wonderland of tantalising ice cream flavours and a haven of delight for families who wanted some normality for their children in the midst of the mayhem and nightly news headlines of bombings and killings.

Wide-eyed children loved spending time checking out all the 21 flavours on display before deciding which one they would spend their weekly pocket money on. A twin cone of 'Blue Surprise' and 'Rubble Bubble' was a particular favourite.

(Pacemaker Press)

Detectives surveying the crime scene on the night of Tuesday, 11 October 1988, shortly after John was murdered and two innocent, ice cream-loving teenagers were callously shot and seriously wounded.

During the four hours following John's murder a total of 22 police and forensics specialists visited Barnam's, including two Chief Superintendents, two Superintendents, a Chief Inspector and four Inspectors.

I naively anticipated that the deployment of so many specialists and experienced officers would produce swift results and convictions. How wrong I was.

Local radio and television news broadcasts reported John's murder continuously in the days following his death. Everywhere we looked we were confronted with newspaper headlines and reports about what happened in Barnam's that night. Many inaccurate.

Telephone
BELFAST 650222

SIR JOHN HERMON, O.B.E., Q.P.M.
CHIEF CONSTABLE

BROOKLYN
KNOCK ROAD
BELFAST
NORTHERN IRELAND BT5 6LE

13 October 1988

Dear Mr. & Mrs. Larmour,

The tragic death of your son on Tuesday was a saddening experience for me, his colleagues and all law abiding people in the Province.

John's death in such callous circumstances has been a dreadful shock and I would wish you to know that all his friends in the Royal Ulster Constabulary and Royal Ulster Constabulary Reserve fully appreciate and share in your grief and sorrow at this sad time.

John was serving the community by making his own contribution to the restoration of peace in Northern Ireland and his death leaves both the police service and the public so much the poorer.

You may be assured that we will always be on hand to help you and your family in every way possible.

You are very much in my thoughts and prayers at this time.

Yours sincerely,

J. Hermon.

Chief Constable

Chief Constable, Sir John Hermon's letter to my Mum and Dad, which was hand-delivered by a member of his staff two days after John was murdered. His reassuring comment that the RUC/PSNI "will always be on hand to help" is not something I have experienced during my 27 years of asking them questions that they, and their Historical Enquiries Team (HET), have deliberately avoided answering.

(Pacemaker Press)

John's son, my nephew Gavin, had his teenage years and future with his Dad cruelly stolen by evil men with blind, blood-splattered hatred in their hearts for someone they never knew or took the time to know. Men who gave no thought to their victim's family, who were left behind to pick up the pieces of their shattered lives.

Gavin has campaigned tirelessly and publicly for justice for his Dad. I hope one day his efforts will be rewarded.

When all the mourners had gone home, John's grave looked very lonely. Over the past 27 years the surrounding ground has been filled by other graves, many of people much younger than John and, sadly, even some children.

THE ICE-CREAM MAN

raisin, vanilla, butter-scotch, walnut, peach:
I rhyme off the flavours. That was before
ered the ice-cream man on the Lisburn Road
ught carnations to lay outside his shop.
you all the wild flowers of the Burren
one day: thyme, valerian, loosestrife,
, tway blade, crowfoot, ling, angelica,
arjoram, cow parsley, sundew, vetch,
, wood sage, ragged robin, stitchwort,
edstraw, bindweed, bog pimpernel

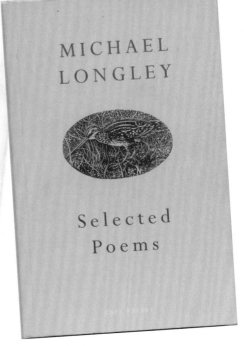

Dear Mr Larmour

It mattered a great deal
to me that we were able
to talk in Waterstone's
a few weeks ago. Here,
as I promised, is my Selected
Poems. The elegy for your
brother is on P. 102. I would
be grateful to learn about
your mother who wrote me
a beautiful heartbreaking
letter about the elegy.

Yours sincerely

Michael Longley

BRIAN BALLARD - 1988
"Poppies in White Jug"
Oil on Board 30" x 24"

MICHAEL
LONGLEY

Selected
Poems

After John was murdered the distinguished poet, Michael Longley, wrote the poem "The Ice-Cream Man" for his young daughter Sarah who was a regular customer in Barnam's. In her innocence she didn't see John as an off-duty policeman, someone to hate. Like many local children who loved Barnam's and its magical ice creams, she couldn't understand why anyone would want to kill 'the ice cream man'.

(Portrait image of Michael Longley courtesy of Colin Davidson)

Over the past 27 years I have written many letters to newspaper editors asking so many questions, demanding answers and seeking the truth.

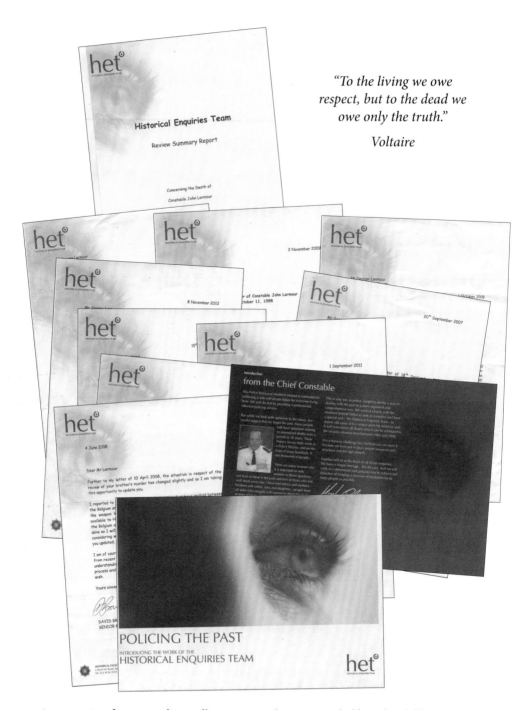

> *"To the living we owe respect, but to the dead we owe only the truth."*
>
> *Voltaire*

A mountain of paperwork – endless, meaningless reports, half-truths, deliberate lies and cover-ups from the RUC, HET, PSNI and Police Ombudsman over the past 27 years that managed to keep the truth hidden from my family. Many victims' families are still searching for the truth surrounding the murders of their loved ones many years after they were brutally maimed and killed.

I believe my brother was sacrificed so that a "Super Tout" could be recruited at the top table of the IRA Army Council. I believe faceless and nameless men in RUC Special Branch protected killers, played God and decided who should live or die, and are as guilty as the gunmen who pulled the triggers.

John Larmour
Born 7 September 1946
Murdered 11 October 1988

"To the living we owe respect but to the dead we owe only the truth." – *Voltaire*

visit the family made to the square in Roermond, where they laid a wreath. He said that Stephen's family had found that visit particularly moving, given that they were seeing, for the first time, the place where their son Stephen and his friend Nick had died.

Ross then divulged that he and the production crew were planning to confront individuals linked to the murders. He had carried out detailed research prior to his visit to Northern Ireland, and knew where to find the people he wanted to speak to. I was curious to hear more but he did not elaborate, so I had to content myself with the knowledge that I would find out what his plans entailed in due course.

I didn't have long to wait. On Sunday, 5 September 2010 I saw an article in the *Sunday Tribune* newspaper by their Northern Editor, Suzanne Breen. Headlined "IRA Past Catches up with Mum", the piece was accompanied by a large photograph of a woman in a car. Her identity was made clear in the subheading, which read "Former double-murder suspect Donna Maguire confronted by an Australian film crew at school gates".

The text of the article related how former IRA bomber, Donna Maguire, once dubbed the most wanted female terrorist in Europe, had been confronted in Newry by an Australian film crew making a documentary about the 1990 murders of Stephen and Nick in Holland. It went on to provide the background to those murders, the arrest weeks later of Donna Maguire in a forest close to the Belgian–Dutch border and the subsequent arrests of her three male associates. Suzanne Breen confirmed that Australia's Channel 7 television company would be airing a new documentary that day. In the course of the programme they would be alleging that British intelligence had had advance knowledge of the murderous attack but had failed to act to prevent it, because, it would also be alleged, they needed to protect possible informers in the IRA team.

The piece described how investigative journalist, Ross Coulthart had confronted Mrs Maguire as she sat in her car, waiting to pick her children up from school. He asked her if she had anything to say about the murders of the two innocent Australians in Holland, assuring her all the while that he had spoken to the Dutch prosecutor and that there was no chance of her ever being prosecuted again in connection to these murders. This was simply an opportunity for her to tell her side of the story. Maguire had nothing to say. It seemed that she had looked genuinely shocked by the confrontation, and drove off without speaking. As she did so, Coulthart asked her if she had ever thought her IRA past would catch up with her.

The report then related how the Melrose family had travelled with Ross Coulthart and the Australian television crew to Donegal to meet a former member of the West Belfast brigade of the IRA, Tommy Gorman. I had read many newspaper articles, books and watched numerous documentaries on our Troubles over the previous 40 odd years, and it wasn't the first time I had read or heard Gorman's name. It now seemed that, on hearing of Gerry Adams' refusal to meet the Melrose family, Tommy Gorman had agreed to speak with them.

During that meeting with the Melroses at his home in Donegal, he gave them background information on the events that led to him joining the IRA. He spoke of how he had witnessed the early riots of the Troubles back in 1969, and how his Catholic community was discriminated against by the majority Unionist government, and badly treated by the RUC. He related how he himself was beaten by members of the RUC and how he had felt compelled to resist the attacks on his community by joining the ranks of the IRA.

Although not directly associated himself with the murders in Holland of the Melroses' innocent son, Stephen and his friend Nick Spanos, Tommy Gorman indicated that it had made no sense for the IRA to kill two innocent tourists, and that it had been a tragic case of mistaken identity that should never have happened. He asserted that Stephen's family deserved to be treated better than they had been, in terms of the refusal of Gerry Adams to meet them.

The article concluded by suggesting that the Melrose family did receive some sense of understanding and indeed comfort from the meeting they had with Tommy Gorman in Donegal. I of course have no right to question who any grieving family should talk to in their own personal quest for answers, the truth and some sort of closure.

At the end of the meeting at Tommy Gorman's home, Stephen's mum Beverly had apparently noted how beautiful the flowers growing in his garden were. He responded by picking a selection of these flowers and giving them to her. This act, of giving flowers to Mrs Melrose, reminded me of little Sarah Longley's own simple gesture when she bought carnations with her ice cream pocket money, because the IRA had killed "the ice cream man" – and of that wreath of remembrance poem her father had written for her and John after my brother was murdered.

Chapter Thirty-Three

Sunday Sequence

I'm not, as I have said, a deeply religious person. I'm uncertain about what I should or should not believe in. I don't know where "up there" is, when people refer to Heaven. But for some inexplicable reason I do enjoy quietly listening to debates on radio about God, and how people feel their life has been helped by their faith. I suppose, deep down, I'm probably looking for something more than my own "as long as you're happy" approach to life and its complexities.

I remember listening to a *Sunday Sequence* radio programme on BBC Radio Ulster on 3 October 2010, just days before the 22nd anniversary of John's murder. The programme featured an item by local author, newspaper and broadcast journalist, Malachi O'Doherty, which involved a discussion about the fact that some of the families of people, who had been killed by the IRA as supposed informers during the Troubles, were seeking more information about the reasons their loved ones were murdered. As part of the item O'Doherty was speaking to the family of Terry Herdman, who had been killed by the IRA over 40 years earlier for being what they termed a "tout". As I listened to the heartbreaking story, as told by the then girlfriend of Mr Herdman, I could understand only too well the anguish and the unanswered questions.

Malachi O'Doherty then introduced another interviewee – Tommy Gorman – to the debate, explaining that Tommy was a self-confessed former member of the IRA. Hearing his name and remembering that he was the person who, a few months earlier, had given flowers from his garden in Donegal to Mrs Melrose, I listened with greater attention.

Since hearing of his meeting with the Melrose family, I had been interested enough to find out a little more about Tommy Gorman's back story. In recent years, he had made several public pronouncements about how he had felt compelled to join the IRA not long after the Divis Street riots in 1969, and how he had been arrested in late 1971. He had talked about his subsequent imprisonment on the Maidstone prison ship, and how he and other IRA comrades had escaped from the Maidstone in 1972. He had generally been very open about his background as a seasoned IRA member over many years. I knew that in more recent times, Gorman had become disgruntled with the direction Sinn Féin had taken throughout the peace process. He had been an outspoken critic of the party and of Gerry Adams, the Sinn Féin president.

So I listened attentively to *Sunday Sequence*, as Tommy Gorman admitted to the family of Terry Herdman the extent of his role in the IRA, while clarifying that he hadn't had any active involvement in that specific operation. He used those same well-rehearsed words and phrases that I had heard him and other self-confessed IRA members use on numerous occasions. He talked about "accepting indirect collective responsibility", and admitted that, like many young people, he had been "easily persuaded" to do certain things by others, and had "tacitly agreed" at the time with the actions he was being asked to perform. He also indicated his "shame" at not "questioning things more strongly" back then, and at just being willing to do what he acknowledged now were "terrible things".

Malachi O'Doherty even went as far as to verbalise his own impression that Tommy Gorman accepted that he had, "uncomfortable memories of a life that [he] could have put to better use", and that at the time he maybe didn't think more about the families concerned. In response to Malachi's question as to whether he had any regrets, Gorman didn't hesitate in answering, "I regret every minute of it."

I must admit that, as I listened, I wondered if that very broad statement, "I regret every minute of it" extended to such actions as the murder of RUC officers like my brother John, and the pain and suffering thereby inflicted to every one of their respective mothers and families.

I understand that everyone's tears are the same. I'm sure the tears of the mother of a dead IRA, INLA, UDA or UVF member are no different from my own mum's tears. All murders are wrong. I have no argument with the many heartbroken mums left behind, no matter who their sons or daughters were. And I would not wish to appear to be trying to explain to a person such as Tommy Gorman how it feels to have a close family member or friend murdered. From my extensive reading, I already know of his thoughts and emotions about the killing of his own friends and the comrades who also chose the path he took.

For example, in Jonathan Stevenson's book, *We Wrecked the Place*, (The

Free Press, 1996), Gorman explains that he was shattered by the deaths of the Gibraltar Three and in particular, by the killing of Dan McCann, his best friend, a man he knew "extraordinarily well" and someone with whom he had been "on the blanket" in prison. Gorman says that the old adage about "being one of nature's gentlemen" was true of his friend, Big Dan McCann and calls McCann "a gentle man", who was religious in his own way and also very funny.

But I'm sure even Tommy Gorman, on reflection, would agree that the random, unconnected killing of my brother John a few months later by the Belfast Brigade of the Provisional IRA didn't provide any meaningful or lasting satisfaction for the person who pulled the trigger, or for the family of Dan McCann. Killing my brother didn't bring Mrs McCann her son back, and my brother's murder didn't further the path to a united Ireland. The truth is that my brother's murder was a waste. It served no purpose. Like all the others, John's murder was simply wrong and ultimately just another pointless bloody footstep along that long, blood-splattered walk to Stormont. Lives and years wasted, for nothing but heartache.

In Stevenson's book, Tommy Gorman addresses the fact that the bombings and shootings he helped perpetrate on behalf of the IRA might have killed people. He goes on to say that if any innocents died on his account, he regrets the loss of life. He then discusses the killing by stabbing of named individuals by Loyalist paramilitaries, commenting that in his view stabbing someone is very personal, and as such, something he could never do. He asserts that "mov[ing] to hit a Brit or RUC [member]" was a very impersonal act, because he was shooting at a uniform. This is a remarkable statement from Gorman, considering he also admits in the same book that one of his brothers was once a member of the British Army, while another was a member of the RUC before the 1969 Troubles erupted.

I wish that I could have been a participant in that edition of *Sunday Sequence* that day. I would have talked about John, my brother, a man just like Tommy Gorman's own brother, who also chose to join the RUC. I would have talked about the fact that John was off-duty and not wearing his police uniform that night in Barnam's. About a killing carried out by the IRA, which was very, very personal. About how someone had decided that my brother deserved to be killed that night, and that his life would be ended by a Speed Six Ruger. The same Ruger that was used to kill Stephen Melrose in Holland, a young man whose mother Tommy Gorman gave flowers to in his Donegal garden.

Chapter Thirty-Four

The Usual Suspects

It seems that many of the best stories feature the number 'seven' in some shape or form. There's the *Magnificent Seven, Seven Brides for Seven Brothers,* the Seven Deadly Sins, the Seven Wonders of the World, and so on. Even the story of Snow White wouldn't be the same without her seven small "hi-ho" friends. Perhaps it's not strange then, that there were seven individuals named in police files as having a possible association with my brother's murder. While as I have said, I was aware from literally the first week after John's death that the police had names, I obviously did not know who these suspects were or how many of them investigators had in their sights. I would have to wait many years before being privy to such details.

The following information was eventually supplied to me by the Historical Enquiries Team in their third report in 2009, and only after I had cajoled and harassed them relentlessly. This report refers to both "suspects" and in more politically correct, law enforcement jargon, "persons of interest". For the sake of simplicity, I will use the term "suspects".

As I have said, I had not been aware before reading the HET report, that the original RUC team of detectives assigned to John's murder had quickly identified seven potential suspects. These were pinpointed through a combination of ordinary police work on the ground by the RUC and reliable intelligence, obtained perhaps from informers within the Belfast Brigade of the Provisional IRA.

Suspect 1 was considered to be the chocolate-loving gunman who shot and killed John at the counter in Barnam's that night, using the Speed Six Ruger .357 Magnum Revolver. This suspect's name was included in intelligence reports obtained by that RUC investigation team soon after the murder. Suspect 1 was arrested in early January 1989 and was subjected to a series of intensive interviews over a three-day period. He refused to speak during interview, and was released without charge.

Suspect 2 was considered to be the gunman who, brandishing the

Browning 9 mm, callously shot and injured the two innocent teenage customers whose only crime that night was their love of Barnam's ice cream. This man was also named in intelligence reports obtained by the RUC investigation team at the same time as they were informed of the name of his comrade, Suspect 1.

Suspect 2 was arrested along with Suspect 1 in January 1989 and also subjected to intensive interviews over that same three-day period. He similarly refused to speak during this time, and was released without charge.

Suspect 3 was, surprisingly, never arrested by the original investigation team, despite the fact that he was named in specific intelligence given to the RUC as being a senior PIRA member, who had provided transport for the two gunmen on the night of John's murder. There are a number of possible reasons why he was never arrested back in 1988. A recent investigation carried out by the Office of the Police Ombudsman for Northern Ireland confirmed that the reliable intelligence surrounding Suspect 3 was not passed on to the original investigation team. And that therefore an important investigative opportunity was missed.

This apparently deliberate withholding of the intelligence surrounding Suspect 3 could have been designed to prevent his arrest and in doing so, to protect him, for whatever reason. Or it is possible that arresting Suspect 3 could have revealed the real source of the intelligence, and that this informer had to be protected at all costs.

Suspect 4, a male with links to the Provisional IRA, was arrested shortly after the murder. He was in a vehicle that was stopped and searched at an Ulster Defence Regiment checkpoint operating in the area that night. Suspect 4 was taken into custody and interviewed about the murder, but also released without charge.

Suspect 5, another male, was also a passenger in the vehicle that was stopped at the UDR checkpoint that night, but he was not arrested.

Suspect 6, a female with links to the Provisional IRA, was already in police custody at the time of the murder for another matter. She was interviewed by police about her knowledge of the murder of my brother John, but no meaningful evidence was obtained during those interviews.

It is difficult to comprehend that, despite so much intelligence being available to the original investigating team, and with so many potential "suspects/persons of interest" being quickly named and/or arrested, held in custody and interviewed, no charges were ever brought. And as we know, even today, many years later, no one has ever been brought to justice for John's murder.

Senior RUC officers, who were involved in the original murder investigation and who could no doubt throw further light on events, declined the invitation to cooperate with the Historical Enquiries Team in the cold case review of John's murder. I had to accept that some former RUC officers didn't like what the HET was set up to do. It was their prerogative to withhold their cooperation from an organisation that was ultimately going to be analysing their original investigative failings and perhaps criticising the difficult work they as over-worked RUC officers were involved in during the many years of the Troubles.

One of these senior investigators, a Detective Inspector, even declined my personal request, made through the HET, for an informal and unofficial meeting with me. This was a request for a casual discussion, so that I, a family member and the brother of one of his murdered RUC colleagues, could somehow try to find out the truth. However, this man said he didn't wish to get involved, and that he had little memory of the events surrounding the murder anyway. A puzzling answer, considering his direct involvement in the original murder investigation. The same man was present at the autopsy of my brother at Belfast City Mortuary on 12 October 1988. He officially identified John's body for the State Pathologist. All I wanted was a non-judgemental chat with him, some help if possible in making sense of the murder and perhaps some much-needed closure.

Suspect 7 entered the proceedings on 1 November 1992, four years after John's murder. He voluntarily walked into Queen's Street Police Station in Belfast that day and asked to speak to a senior officer. He said he wanted to provide information and said that it related to his involvement in a number of serious, terrorist-related offences, including the murder of Constable John Larmour in Barnam's Ice Cream Parlour in 1988. He was immediately arrested under the Prevention of Terrorism Act and subjected to a series of interviews about his confessions. The Detective Inspector, who was part of the original murder investigation, and who declined my request for a casual meeting, was also the person who dealt with Suspect 7, a man who apparently wished to confess his sins. A total of ten other officers were also involved in the interviews which followed.

During these interviews Suspect 7 correctly named Suspects 1 and 2, and implicated them as being the two gunmen who carried out the murder of

Constable Larmour. He also accurately described one of the weapons that was used during the murder as a Browning 9 mm.

Suspect 7 also claimed that three weeks before the murder, he was asked by a known member of the IRA to visit Barnam's as a customer, with the specific task of looking for a wedding cake that was supposedly on display inside the parlour. He said that this senior IRA member told him that the wedding cake, instead of having the traditional little bride and groom figures on its top tier, would have miniature figures of a male police officer and a female officer, both in RUC uniform. The IRA member told him that the presence of this wedding cake inside Barnam's would confirm that the ice cream parlour was in fact owned by a married couple who were also serving members of the RUC.

Suspect 7 went on to say that the IRA member stated that if this information was confirmed, then the male officer would be shot in retaliation for the fatal shootings of Sean Savage and Dan McCann by the SAS in Gibraltar in March 1988. He also stated that if the policewoman was there, she would be shot alongside her husband, in retaliation for the shooting dead of Mairéad Farrell by the SAS during that Gibraltar operation.

Suspect 7 then said that he had visited Barnam's as instructed and had reported back to the senior IRA member that he had seen a two-tiered wedding cake, with small RUC-uniformed male and female figures on top, on display inside the parlour during his reconnaissance visit. He then went on to say that Suspect 1 (the chocolate-loving gunman) had subsequently carried out the murder in the ice cream parlour in October 1988.

As previously mentioned, my wife and I were of course the official owners and operators of Barnam's World of Ice Cream. The suggestion that we would personally display or allow to be displayed inside our shop in 1988, a wedding cake featuring RUC-uniformed bride and groom figures, is a ludicrous one. Not only because neither of us had any involvement in the RUC, but also, and perhaps more importantly, because of the potential security implications for us and the various, mostly female, staff we employed, who came from both the Roman Catholic and Protestant traditions. To do such a thing during this era of the Troubles in Belfast would have been madness.

No such police-themed wedding cake was ever displayed or even briefly taken into Barnam's or shown to any staff members there. No photographs of any such cake were ever displayed in Barnam's or shown to any staff members. So if Suspect 7 reported back to the senior IRA member that he had seen such a thing during his reconnaissance mission, he was clearly not telling his contact the truth.

However it is significant that, according to Suspect 7's account, the senior IRA contact was able to mention this police-themed wedding cake at all. He was obviously aware of the existence of such a cake from some other source, and keen to connect it with Barnam's to back up his knowledge. For, although it was never displayed publicly in our parlour at any time, my brother and his wife did indeed have a wedding cake like this at their marriage reception, with two tiny RUC-uniformed figures on the top tier instead of a traditional bride and groom.

My brother had married a second time in May 1987, the year before he was murdered. During the wedding reception, the couple had briefly had the traditional bride and groom figures on the top tier of their wedding cake replaced with two RUC-uniformed officer figures. A photograph had been taken of this police-themed version of their wedding cake and was included in their secondary, private wedding album, along with other traditional wedding photographs taken on the day.

Many would suggest that this replacing of the traditional bride and groom figures on the cake with RUC figures was a risky thing to do. I would not disagree with that interpretation. It was indeed a foolhardy action on the part of two serving RUC members, who should have considered the security implications of a public display of this kind – even such a brief one – at their wedding reception. In hindsight, it would have been better if they had not compromised their safety with this unnecessary display of light-hearted bravado, and I personally questioned their judgement at the time.

But the really important question in all of this is, how did the senior IRA member, who asked Suspect 7 to visit Barnam's, know about the police-themed cake? My own investigations point to a possible explanation and an additional "person of interest".

During 1987 and 1988, both my brother and his new wife regularly visited a particular retail outlet. It was an establishment that at the time was considered safe for them and other serving police officers to frequent. I know that John's wife took her small, private wedding album into this place during 1987 to show to some female members of staff. Unfortunately, she forgot to remove the private photograph showing the wedding cake with the two uniformed figures on the top. I am also aware that during their visits to this retail outlet, both John and his new wife mentioned the opening of Barnam's World of Ice Cream and the family connection.

I am led to believe that, unknown to either John or his wife, there was a female member of staff working in that retail outlet at the time, who was intimately connected to a known IRA member in West Belfast. I wonder – although this is something which I cannot prove – if it is possible that this female staff member passed on the information about the incriminating wedding cake photograph to that IRA member and others, after she had seen the small wedding album in 1987?

Armed with this vital piece of information about a police husband and wife, did the IRA file this intelligence away for future consideration? Did they monitor the situation and try to build up additional intelligence concerning this police couple? To act immediately on the wedding cake photograph information, and target either John or his new wife separately or together at the retail outlet in question would obviously have alerted police to the possibility that a staff member there had set them up for assassination. Were the IRA therefore keen to establish the couple's habitual movements, in order to be able to target them at a less incriminating location than the original retail outlet?

Perhaps time and careful monitoring proved effective when the necessary additional information presented itself, and both John and his new wife spoke about their family connection to the new Barnam's World of Ice Cream parlour that was opening on the Lisburn Road in July 1988 – a location that was within a relatively short driving distance of the base of the Belfast Brigade of the IRA in the west of the city. Such a location would allow for a well-planned ambush operation to be set up, culminating in the murder or murders of police officers and would enable the swift passage of the hit team back to safe houses in West Belfast.

At a certain point during those 1992 interviews, Suspect 7 was examined by a doctor, who prescribed sedatives and declared him unfit for further interview. He was subsequently admitted to the psychiatric wing of a local hospital.

On 10 November 1993 a comprehensive report detailing the admissions of Suspect 7, including his involvement in the murder of my brother John, was submitted by an RUC Detective Inspector to the Director of Public Prosecutions, with a recommendation that Suspect 7 be charged with my brother John's murder and other offences he admitted to. But the following July, the DPP ruled that there was to be no prosecution of Suspect 7 at that time.

Despite his credible admissions and his correct naming of Suspects 1 and 2 back in 1992, Suspect 7 has never been charged. I have concerns that Suspect 7 was removed from police custody to a psychiatric unit for reasons of strategy and convenience, and that he was never charged in order to protect a more important source within the IRA that he, Suspect 7, would be able to identify.

In 2009, in the course of their so-called in-depth cold case review of my brother's murder, I asked the HET if they intended re-arresting Suspect 7, to ascertain if he was still willing to make those admissions and to determine whether or not his current mental state was such that any repeat admissions he made could be deemed reliable, and subsequent charges be issued.

The HET were willing to tell me that Suspect 7 was still alive (which is still the case as this book goes to print), that they were aware of his current whereabouts and activities, and that he would appear to be functioning normally in society. They however refused to comment on his current mental state, citing the fact that personal medical records are subject to conditions of strict confidentiality. But they did conclude by saying that they felt that Suspect 7's current reliability as a witness might still be deemed questionable.

Obviously unhappy with their assumption, I stated that their decision was not based on a recognised medical psychiatric assessment of Suspect 7. I told them that I did not accept their conclusion that they "felt" that he "might" not be reliable as a witness. I suggested that, based on the information they had been willing to supply about his current life, his capacity as a witness was worthy of reassessment. I said that I wanted his mental capacity to be assessed by an appropriate medical professional as a precursor to formal arrest and questioning about his previous, credible admissions of guilt in my brother's murder. He should at least be capable of undergoing a fresh interview, which would give him the opportunity to revisit those admissions, so that any information he was able and willing to provide could be taken into account. The HET refused my request in 2009 and gave no plausible reason for doing so.

So many questions remain. Why in 1992 was Suspect 7 conveniently moved to a psychiatric ward, within hours of his credible and accurate confession, and never charged with any offence in relation to his confession of involvement in John's murder? Why, in recent years, have the HET refused to investigate this evidential line of enquiry?

And most importantly of all, why do so many people not want the truth about the murder of my brother to come out?

Chapter Thirty-Five

Double Standards

In 2012, I read with interest reports in the local media of the arrest on 11 October that year of someone accused of assisting in the 1993 murder of Constable Michael Ferguson in Londonderry. According to these articles, this person's defence lawyers had cited the defendant's history of serious mental health problems, evidenced by the fact that he had been a patient in Gransha Mental Health Hospital 15 times during the previous four years. Despite this, however, the Police Service of Northern Ireland had felt that an arrest was appropriate on his most recent discharge from hospital.

It seemed that this same person had made a series of admissions to police in 2008, but had then retracted these statements. During a recent stay in hospital, the police were constantly in contact with him. The man's lawyer indicated that when his client had been arrested in 2012, a doctor who examined him inside a police station had pronounced that he was not fit to be interviewed. However, a detective inspector said that the man had later been examined by a psychiatrist, who deemed him well enough to be questioned. It seemed that the man had then gone on to give a very detailed account relating to the murder of Constable Michael Ferguson and a number of other terrorist incidents. The detective inspector said he had no doubts about the defendant's credibility or about his involvement in these incidents.

I must admit that I felt mixed emotions at reading about this latest development in another historical case involving the murder of another RUC officer. I was pleased by the determination of the police officers carrying out the investigation to pursue justice for Constable Ferguson and his family after so many years. A determination which contrasted starkly with the lack of commitment on the part of the Historical Enquiries Team in their cold case review of John's murder.

Even in the course of their inadequate investigations, the HET had stated that after reviewing the 1992 interviews of Suspect 7, it was clear that he knew relevant facts surrounding John's murder, and about those directly and indirectly involved. Yet here I was now, reading about someone who had made admissions and had mental health problems, and was being arrested in connection with the murder of an RUC officer many years before. Despite my demand for the same process to be considered, the HET had refused to contemplate such a course of action.

I therefore requested that the PSNI and HET look at this aspect of my brother's murder investigation again. On 2 November 2012 I wrote to the then Chief Constable of the PSNI, Mr Matt Baggott and the Director of the Historical Enquiries Team, Mr David Cox and requested they re-arrest Suspect 7, to put to him in interview the admissions he voluntarily made back in 1992, asking him to confirm, deny, or elaborate on those admissions. I demanded that he should be assessed professionally by proper psychiatric personnel to establish his current mental state and potential reliability as a witness. I said I didn't know if Suspect 7 had been admitted as a psychiatric patient in recent years but, even if he had, as witnessed by the recent arrest in Constable Ferguson's case, that should not be a barrier to an arrest now.

In this way, at least something positive would have been done for our family in terms of the justice my brother and my late mum and dad, and all of us deserved. I said that in the recent arrest associated with Constable Ferguson's murder, I saw many striking similarities with the circumstances of the murder of my own brother. And that, unlike in Constable Ferguson's case, in this instance Suspect 7 had never retracted his original admissions. They were still credible and still on record.

I reiterated in my letter that I was certain that the family of Constable Ferguson would be heartened by this latest development in relation to their loved one's murder, even many years later. This recent arrest might bring them some sort of sense of justice and some sort of closure, but also showed them that someone cared enough about their pain to at least try every avenue of investigation available. I said I was sure they accepted that there would be no guarantee of a positive outcome. I told Mr Baggott and Mr Cox that I could not allow the premature deaths of my mum and dad from grief to simply become silent statistics of our so-called Troubles, nor could I allow my brother's murder to go unpunished, simply because those whose job it was to pursue the perpetrators seemed to want for whatever reason to hide the truth.

I concluded by asking that they take my request seriously and said that I looked forward to their carefully considered reply. I hand-delivered the letters that very day, 2 November, to the offices of the Chief Constable and the HET, and began to think about my next move while awaiting their reply.

§

On 7 November 2012, I received a one-page, two-line response from Police Headquarters, informing me that the Chief Constable thanked me for my letter, and that it was receiving attention. The letter was signed by Inspector Andrew S Campbell on behalf of the Chief Constable.

Around the same time, I was contacted by my senior contact within the HET, David Brown, who told me that he had been instructed by Police Headquarters to respond to my letter. He invited me to attend a meeting at HET headquarters at Sprucefield.

I duly attended this meeting, and there David Brown outlined the HET's position. He started by saying that, although he was aware of the ongoing PSNI case in relation to the murder of Constable Ferguson, he was not familiar with the fine detail of this investigation. He acknowledged that there appeared to be similarities between the Ferguson investigation and circumstances relating to the person referred to as Suspect 7 in the investigation of John's murder.

He went on to say however that Suspect 7's case had been thoroughly assessed at the time in 1993 by the Director of Public Prosecutions (DPP), and that it had been ruled that, because of mental health issues, no prosecution would be pursued, and that none of the evidence Suspect 7 provided could be used in relation to the investigation. Therefore, based on that original 1993 decision by the DPP, it would, he concluded, not be possible to take any further action, without being able to demonstrate that any fresh investigation would reveal evidence which was both new and compelling. In his opinion, this was not the situation with Suspect 7, and as such neither the HET nor the PSNI could take any further action.

So re-arresting Suspect 7 was not even being considered by HET or the Chief Constable in 2012, and they did not wish to pursue any new evidential opportunities based on his credible admissions, voluntarily made in 1992. Once more, I had to ask myself the question: why do those, whose job it is to find and assess any potential evidence relating to the murder of my brother, not wish to do so?

Chapter Thirty-Six

Super Tout

On 18 November 2012, just a few weeks after my exchange of letters with the Chief Constable and the HET about Suspect 7, an article appeared in the *Sunday World* newspaper under the headline: "MI5 Paid Cop-Killer £70k to be a Tout". The story was heralded as an "exclusive".

In this piece, the newspaper's editor claimed that a top "Provo" had been paid almost £70,000 to turn "tout", just days after he had taken part in the killing of a policeman in an ice cream parlour. This dynamite claim had apparently been detailed in a dossier that had recently come into possession of the *Sunday World*. In fact, I had had some advance warning that the story was going to break. David Brown of the HET, had spoken to me the previous week and made me aware that the publication of the story was imminent.

The *Sunday World* piece went on to say that the victim of the still unsolved murder was an off-duty RUC officer, John Larmour, who was gunned down in Barnam's ice cream parlour in 1988, and that no one had ever been brought to book for the point-blank murder of Constable Larmour. According to the file which had newly come to light, the article continued, the finger of blame was pointing to a top Provo, now turned "peacemaker" – he had been responsible for firing one of the two lethal weapons used during the ambush on Larmour.

The *Sunday World* said that, while for legal reasons, the alleged killer couldn't be named, the paper was able to reveal that he had served time in prison for bomb and gun-related terrorist crimes, and that he was not only a one-time commander of the Provisional IRA in Belfast, but had also been a member of the PIRA Army Council. Further, this man was apparently one of the former top IRA men who had swung in behind Gerry Adams and the Sinn Féin leadership when they turned from paramilitarism to politics; in recent years he had also been on the frontline of efforts to avert violence at Orange parade interface flashpoints by "engaging" with intermediaries, including representatives of both the Loyalist Ulster Defence Association (UDA) and the Ulster Volunteer Force (UVF).

The article alleged that after the murder, John's killers had fled to a "safe house". Unknown to the Provos, however, it seemed that this property, which had been provided by an estate agent, Joseph Fenton, since killed by the IRA as an informer, had been bugged by MI5. Therefore every word uttered by John's killers and their co-conspirators was recorded. It seemed that anti-terror officers within the RUC, some of whom knew John as a trusted and well-respected colleague, wanted to arrest and charge the suspects, but MI5 allegedly blocked that route. Instead, according to the explosive new dossier in the paper's possession, MI5 "had other plans for the killers of off-duty Constable John Larmour".

According to the file, one of the gunmen was subsequently arrested – "a high-profile PIRA volunteer from West Belfast". He was taken in for questioning in Castlereagh RUC Station in Belfast, the base of the RUC's Special Branch. It seemed that, as this top Provo was being interviewed by the police, the MI5 tape of him talking in the "safe house" was played to him. At this point, according to the *Sunday World*, "a suitcase was opened and inside it was £67,000, which was the top Provo's 'incentive' to work for the Intelligence/Security services, along with the promise of no prosecution for the murder of Constable John Larmour".

The senior IRA man apparently agreed to take the money, and he "turned tout" just like other senior republicans before him, including Denis Donaldson and Freddie Scappaticci. The damning dossier claimed that the killer said to his interviewers, in response to their offer, "What do you want to know?", and that he "took the Queen's shilling" and went on to become a highly paid informer within the upper echelons of the Provisional IRA. As part of this new role, he allegedly was allowed to continue killing, in order to protect his cover as a British agent.

Finally, the dossier also linked a gun – a Ruger, used in the murder of Constable John Larmour – to a previous killing: that of Colin Abernethy, a founder member and Treasurer of the Ulster Clubs organisation, who was shot dead on a Belfast-bound train on 9 September 1988.

This supposedly "exclusive" super tout dossier story also managed to make its way onto the pages of the *Sunday World's* rival paper, the *Sunday Life* that same weekend. The *Sunday Life* also declined to name the alleged super tout, no doubt for legal reasons as well. It quoted equally unidentified "security sources", who predicted that the name of the top Provo who gunned down John Larmour would emerge soon after the newspaper revelations. This paper cited one veteran source, who pronounced, "This guy is a key agent at the heart of the IRA in Belfast. He was MI5's man on the Army Council", and went on to say that the same man's information saved lives, but that he was also involved in the taking of other lives in order to retain his position of authority at the top of the IRA. The article also stated that in 1998, this top Provo had played a crucial role in encouraging the IRA to support power-sharing at Stormont. Although up until then he had been considered a "hawk" who favoured continuing with the terror campaign, he had surprisingly switched allegiances in 1998, defecting to a faction headed by Gerry Adams that was steering a course towards government at Stormont. Apparently the same individual had remained a key Adams' ally on the IRA Army Council, right up until the decommissioning of PIRA weapons and explosives in 2005. Thereafter this top informant had kept a fairly low-profile and rarely ventured out of his west Belfast home. He was still a Sinn Féin supporter and had resisted overtures to join dissident organisations.

The only real point of difference between the two rival papers' coverage of this story related to the *Sunday Life's* "low profile" remark in talking of the "top Provo's" recent activities, whereas the *Sunday World* stated that he had been seen at interface demonstrations in recent years, apparently playing the role of "peacemaker" during contentious Orange Order parades.

Within weeks of John's murder, I had been aware of the possible involvement of an informer who was being protected by elements of the security forces. I was of course never able to confirm this suspicion, or the identity of this individual. However I would be very surprised if veteran IRA operators and current Sinn Féin members – including Sinn Féin President, Gerry Adams and deputy First Minister, Martin McGuinness – were unable to identify the figure those Sunday newspaper articles were referring to. It wouldn't require any kind of sophisticated code-breaking facility to enable former comrades and associates to join the dots and come up with a name. Or, failing that, they could simply draw up a list of names of Army Council members and crossmatch the various details to arrive at that person's identity.

However, it is my belief that the *Sunday World* and *Sunday Life* reports contained a significant error, in suggesting that the super tout was one of the two gunmen who entered Barnam's and murdered John and wounded the two teenage customers: the two gunmen who are referred to as Suspect 1 and

Suspect 2 by the Historical Enquiries Team. In fact I have been informed by my HET contacts that super tout was not one of the two gunmen that night in Barnam's, and is not Suspect 1 or Suspect 2 as suggested. It is my belief however that this senior Provo was directly responsible for the meticulous planning of John's murder, including details such as the selection of the two gunmen and the weapons used.

Given his important role in John's murder, it seems very likely that he would also have been taken to the safe house, along with the two gunmen. It is therefore likely that MI5/RUC Special Branch recorded the conversations of all three IRA members who were involved in John's murder in the safe house that night – and the conversations too perhaps of other members who provided back-up and transport.

In the following weeks, as you can imagine, I scoured the editions of both Sunday papers thoroughly, but the prediction by the *Sunday Life's* unnamed security sources, that the identity of this "top Provo super tout" would soon emerge, never materialised.

Chapter Thirty-Seven

Dear Mr Baggott – Again

Having carefully analysed both of those Sunday newspaper articles, I felt that my next step should be to write to the Chief Constable again, despite having had no meaningful response to my previous correspondence to him. Bearing in mind the response I had already had from David Brown of the HET, indicating that they could not proceed without any new and compelling evidence, I considered that it was the Chief Constable's job to provide that new evidence.

Mr Baggott,

Further to my letter to you on 2 November 2012, and in light of the articles that appeared in the *Sunday World* and *Sunday Life* newspapers on 18 November 2012, I … insist that the following should be seriously considered by you.

I have always known, from within days after my brother was murdered … [that] there was credible intelligence obtained by the RUC that identified and named the two gunmen directly involved. At the time I was obviously unaware of the actual source of that … intelligence, but suspected it was obtained from an informer within the IRA.

However, on reading the articles in last Sunday's newspapers, it is now becoming clear that … those who were directly involved in murdering my brother, and the person who helped plan and authorise the murder, were taken to at least one [safe house], if not a number of safe houses in West Belfast, supplied to the IRA by local estate agent, Joseph Fenton. And that, unknown to the IRA, those safe houses had been bugged for some considerable period of time by MI5 and/or RUC Special Branch. That the conversations (confessions) of those involved in John's murder were listened to and recorded. And, [that] instead of those involved and implicated in my brother John's murder ... being immediately arrested and charged, someone decided that they would approach the senior member who organised and authorised John's murder, with the intention of turning him into an informer.

It seems that during the days and weeks following John's murder ... this person was confronted with the recorded evidence against him and [was] persuaded to become an informer, with the promise that he would not be charged with John's murder and perhaps with other murders that he also implicated himself in during previously recorded conversations he was involved in at those designated safe houses. It looks like this approach was successful, and indeed this high-ranking IRA member became an informer ...

However, it would appear that to protect him, attention had to be deflected away from him as a possible informer ... So in January 1989, the two gunmen were arrested and brought to Castlereagh RUC Station and interviewed over a three-day period ... Despite their refusal to answer any questions, it appears obvious that they could have been charged with John's murder based on the recorded conversations from the safe houses.

Was their arrest simply a well-choreographed deception and deflection, to ensure that on their release the attention of the IRA's Internal Investigation Department ... would focus its questions towards Joseph Fenton and away from the new, potentially more powerful IRA super tout?

Was Joseph Fenton deemed to have outlived his usefulness as an informer, and was he sacrificed to protect this new super tout? If that was the intention, it certainly worked, because as we all know, weeks later in February 1989 Joseph Fenton was abducted by the IRA and interrogated by their infamous "Nutting Squad". During that interrogation he admitted his role as an informer and the fact that the safe houses he had been supplying were bugged. And as we all know, Joseph Fenton was then shot dead ... and his informer role publicly acknowledged by the IRA. His father ... was provided with, and sadly accepted as being true, his son's confession.

The fact that Joseph Fenton could well have been sacrificed to protect the new super tout is doubly repugnant, when in fact it is highly probable that the person who interrogated him during that two-day period, who tortured him into confessing, and perhaps even killed him, was another long-term, high-ranking informer within the IRA, commonly referred to publicly as "Stakeknife", and allegedly exposed as Freddie Scappaticci. So sacrificing Joseph Fenton ensured that at least two more highly-placed informers were protected and allowed to continue their mayhem as long as they were willing to also act as informers.

Even more crucially, the fact that Joseph Fenton confessed that his safe houses had been bugged before John was murdered, throws up another concern I have about my brother's murder.

I prepared Barnam's for official opening during the period [between] March 1988 until July 1988, when it opened, and John was murdered in October 1988. A very short timeframe. And it's likely that during that … time frame, Joseph Fenton's bugged safe houses would have been in operation. I therefore conclude that it is highly likely that John's murder was actually planned and discussed by those involved in one of those safe houses prior to his murder …

Did MI5 and/or RUC Special Branch actually listen to and record the [details of the] planned attack on my brother? Could they have prevented his murder, but [did they] instead sacrifice him, a fellow RUC officer … because they had a bigger plan in place, to recruit a new super tout within the future IRA Army Council?

So many victims' families here are patronised, in the hope that they will stay silent and hopefully one day will all just give up or die, and will not be around to rock the supposed peace boat.

… The HET's recent reply to the letter I sent to you, and copied to them, was as I suspected: that it is not within their remit to re-arrest Suspect 7 without any new evidence. Therefore I consider it is your job to provide that new evidence, and repeat my requests to you as per my previous letter…

Re-arrest Suspect 7, assess his current mental capability and ask him if he wishes to repeat his credible admissions about his involvement in my brother John's murder, his naming of individuals involved and other accurate information.

Re-arrest Suspect 1 and Suspect 2 … and put to them the recorded conversations that were obtained in the safe houses in October 1988 … And having done so, charge them with John's murder.

Arrest the super tout, and put to him his own recorded admissions … of involvement in John's murder obtained from the safe houses. And having done so, charge him with John's murder.

… I have been deliberately forthright in this letter and have deliberately avoided the politically correct word "alleged" [in relation to my brother's] murderers, because I am no longer willing to play the game of pretending we all don't know the truth. We do, but those who should be telling that truth prefer to hide behind cloaks of secrecy and … misinformation to suit their own agendas.

… I … await your full and detailed written reply to my letters. But more importantly, I look forward to actions as well as words.

George Larmour

Once more I soon received the standard and annoying one-page, two-line note from the Chief Constable's office, thanking me for my second letter and informing me yet again that it was "receiving attention".

I also received a telephone call soon after from David Brown, my senior contact within HET. He informed me that, although he had not seen my second letter to the Chief Constable, he had been informed by Police Headquarters that they were forwarding my second letter to him and had asked him to respond to me.

David Brown was in no doubt about my frustration during that telephone conversation. I told him I was not interested in dealing with him, and that my second letter was not addressed to him. That I expected my second letter to be dealt with by the Chief Constable and no one else. I sent a further letter directly to Mr Matt Baggott, letting him know just how angry I was.

Chapter Thirty-Eight

Passing the Buck

On Saturday, 19 January 2013, I received a further letter from an Inspector Andrew Campbell on behalf of the Chief Constable, addressing the annoyance I had expressed in my third letter to his Chief. Inspector Campbell wrote that he understood my disappointment that my original correspondence was progressed by and to others, rather than being dealt with personally by the Chief Constable. He assured me that my concerns were receiving their full attention and that the Chief Constable was confident that those he had tasked to address the matters contained within my correspondence were best placed to do so and indeed enjoyed the Chief Constable's full support in their task.

Once more, I angrily replied directly to the Chief Constable. I pointed out that it had been four months since I first had written to him personally, but that I had yet to hear anything meaningful in response. I said that latest missive from Inspector Campbell had not advanced the situation one iota, but instead had done nothing more than patronise me with meaningless soundbites: "receiving attention", "best placed to do so", "enjoy his full support", and so on. I concluded by saying that the content of my previous correspondence to him had been unambiguous and was deserving of action, and that I would continue to expect a direct response to my requests from him personally.

In March 2013, a new name entered the correspondence – a Superintendent Ryan Henderson. In his letter he stated that he was responding on Mr Baggott's behalf. He reiterated that he was sorry that I was dissatisfied with the responses I had so far received from the PSNI, and told me that he had reviewed the circumstances to satisfy himself that the most appropriate course of action had been arrived at in trying to deal with my concerns. He stated that he wanted to reassure me that there had never been any desire on the part of the PSNI to treat my requests with contempt, as I had suggested, and that he considered that the steps taken by his colleague, Inspector

Campbell regarding my concerns and correspondence, were appropriate. He concluded by saying that if I remained dissatisfied, then I might wish to refer the matter to the Police Ombudsman for Northern Ireland (PONI), who could conduct an independent review of the PSNI's actions in the matter.

This suggestion – that I might wish to involve the Police Ombudsman's office – felt like a stalling tactic to me: another mechanism by which to deflect my concerns and avoid the Chief Constable having to deal with my correspondence. So I replied as follows – again, directly to the Chief Constable:

Dear Chief Constable,

In reply to the letter sent to me on your behalf by Superintendent Ryan Henderson, dated 22 March 2013, I fully accept the comments being made by him, and appreciate it is reasonable that you might ask others with an in-depth knowledge of the circumstances and the issues I have raised to become involved to progress matters.

However, I also feel it is reasonable that I as a member of a victim's family, who has hand-delivered … numerous letters addressed directly to you since November 2012, [should] expect something more substantial in response …

And I accept that there may have been no deliberate attempt on your part to treat my concerns with the contempt I feel has been displayed, but the complete lack of substance in the replies I have received to date, and the deliberate attempts to pass responsibility over to David Brown at HET to deal with me, have left me with no other option but to feel this way.

Unfortunately this is how many victims' families are feeling here, [despite the fact that] all we ever hear is how important victims and their families supposedly are in the task of dealing with the past.

Considering my correspondence has been addressed to you personally, Mr Baggott, it would be reassuring to not just receive something more tangible in reply, but that one which actually has your signature on it. I am beginning to wonder if you personally have not even had sight of my letters. And if that is the case, then it certainly would be a contemptible situation.

In answer to Superintendent Henderson's PONI suggestion, my answer is "No". I do not wish to refer the matter of my dissatisfaction to the Office of the Police Ombudsman for Northern Ireland. I won't even bother apologising for appearing so cynical, but this quite honestly appears to be simply an easier option for you, in that this will have the desired effect of transferring the responsibility for addressing my legitimate concerns to the PONI office.

I would prefer that you, Mr Baggott, would answer my concerns as addressed to you, the Chief Constable: not to HET and not to PONI – but to you personally.

… I would respectfully ask you as Chief Constable to assure me that you are personally aware of my concerns, and … provide me with reassurance that you are actively planning to [consider] my requests and [give] me a positive indication of when they are likely to be actioned, or of your reasons for refusing to do so.

I look forward to your reply, Chief Constable.

George Larmour

§

Unsurprisingly the Chief Constable did not reply. Instead, on 7 August 2013, I received a further letter from Superintendent Ryan Henderson, which began, predictably, by informing me that he was responding on behalf of Mr Baggott. He explained that he was specifically writing to me this time with regard to my prior reference to information printed in recent Sunday newspaper articles relating to the murder of my brother.

Superintendent Henderson acknowledged my desire that my concerns should be addressed by the Chief Constable and the PSNI, rather than by the Police Ombudsman for Northern Ireland. He went on to say however that, as the matters referred to in my letters and in the Sunday newspaper articles involved the gathering of intelligence, the PSNI, in responding to them, had to comply with United Kingdom national guidelines and accordingly could neither confirm nor deny the claims made in these press articles. As far as I was concerned, this was just another convenient, catch-all method of deflecting my legitimate concerns, and of not having to deal with them head-on.

The Superintendent went on to say that, after having carefully considered the matter, it had been determined that the newspaper articles and my letters did allege possible police misconduct, and that therefore the PSNI were compelled by legislation to refer the matter to the office of the Police Ombudsman for Northern Ireland for further investigation. They had now done this. He then advised me that since, as I had made it clear in my previous correspondence, I did not wish PONI to deal with my concerns, the PSNI's transfer of the material to them would not be treated as an official complaint at this stage. He advised that this would remain the case, unless I made contact directly with PONI.

So, despite me stating that I did not want the Police Ombudsman to deal with my concerns, the Chief Constable and his staff were totally disregarding my wishes. It had taken almost a year of my letters "receiving attention" for me to finally be told that the Chief Constable was never going to answer my concerns anyway. I could have been told that much sooner, but obviously it was easier to string me along for as long as possible, to give the impression that the Chief Constable cared. I suppose it was always clear that his office would ultimately use the "we cannot comment on intelligence matters" card to avoid having to deal with my concerns.

Now they had managed to sweep my letters off the Chief Constable's desk and onto the overloaded desk of the Police Ombudsman for Northern Ireland. Presumably, they hoped that the Police Ombudsman would stick my file at the bottom of his in-tray, and that no one would have to deal with me for another few years. That nuisance brother of a murdered RUC officer was finally dispensed with, and another victim's family member had been dealt with without having to really address their concerns. A scenario which has been all too familiar for so many victims' families in recent times.

Author's note: The man who confessed in 2012 his involvement in the 1993 murder of Constable Ferguson was charged in 2015, tried, found guilty and sentenced to ten years in jail.

Chapter Thirty-Nine

The Silencing of a Lawyer

On Sunday, 12 February 1989, Belfast solicitor Patrick Finucane was sitting with his wife Geraldine and their three young children, enjoying a family meal in the kitchen of their home at Fortwilliam Drive in North Belfast.

The convivial family scene was all at once horribly shattered, as Loyalist gunmen, using a sledgehammer, forced their way into the house and made directly to the kitchen area, where they quickly shot Finucane twice. As he lay injured on the kitchen floor, one of the gunmen stood over him and fired a further 12 shots into his body and face, killing him. His wife was also injured in the attack. Their children, two sons aged 9 and 17, and a daughter aged 12, were uninjured but witnessed the appalling murder of their father.

Ever since the awful events of that night, there has been speculation that the lawyer's killers were aided by members of the security forces. Bit by bit over the years, those suspicions have been confirmed as truth because of the repeated calls from the Finucane family for the facts to be told. However, their demands for a full, independent Public Inquiry into his murder have been continually rejected by the British government. In December 2012, the results of The Pat Finucane Review, carried out by Sir Desmond de Silva, were published, and documented extensive evidence of State collaboration with Loyalist gunmen in Finucane's murder.

On hearing the outcome of the De Silva Review, British Prime Minister, David Cameron acknowledged there had been "shocking levels of collusion" in evidence, and issued a public apology to the Finucane family. However, the family and in particular Pat Finucane's widow, Geraldine, denounced the De Silva Review as a "sham" and a "suppression of the truth", and called for a full Public Inquiry.

I am all in favour of getting to the truth. I know what it feels like to have a loved one murdered. Any family deserves the full, unvarnished truth of how and why their loved one was killed, and who the perpetrator was.

Every family's private tears are ultimately the same. But do I believe that lengthy and costly Public Inquiries, like the Bloody Sunday Inquiry, will provide that full undistorted truth? No, I don't. I feel that such inquiries still leave families with questions which deliberately remain unanswered. And I consider that the monumental expenditure associated with these kinds of inquiries is money which could be spent on more worthwhile things than filling the pockets of highly-paid lawyers.

But I respect the right of any family to demand such an Inquiry, if they feel that is the only avenue towards the truth they seek. Mrs Finucane has publicly indicated that she is not particularly interested in having the names of the gunmen revealed. She feels that they were merely pawns in a much bigger game that was being played out. This begs an important question – what exactly is the truth the Finucane family are so determined to have publicly revealed?

Is it, as most people suspect, to have those within the British Intelligence organisation, MI5, who perhaps colluded with and manipulated the Loyalist gunmen to have Pat Finucane murdered, named and exposed for their dirty dealings with outlawed paramilitary killers? Do the Finucane family want members of the former RUC Special Branch, who they believe conspired with those Loyalist killers, to be named and forced to publicly tell the truth? Or indeed, would they want a Public Inquiry to go even further up the collusion chain of command, and reveal the names of members of the British government who perhaps knew of in advance, and sanctioned, Pat Finucane's murder, possibly even including the Prime Minister at the time, Margaret Thatcher?

All of this begs further important questions. Have the Finucane family's requests for a full Public Inquiry been so consistently refused, because it is judged that the stark truth about all those possible participants, and colluders, in this murder is too explosive to be brought into the public domain? Are there too many prominent figures within all those organisations, whose protection is deemed more important than the truth being told?

I don't doubt there are people within those security and intelligence organisations and the British Government perhaps, who would wish their identities to remain secret. However, I believe it is possible that there is another, equally important name that needs to be kept from the public, and another significant reason why the Finucane family cannot be told the full, undistorted truth.

Here's my own theory. I'm not saying it is correct; I cannot prove it. But in the clandestine, "smoke-and-mirrors" world of MI5 spooks, RUC Special Branch, informants and handlers, it's as credible as any other hypothesis.

My brother John was an unconnected, but easy target for members of the West Belfast brigade of the IRA, who wanted to avenge the deaths of their friends and IRA comrades in Gibraltar in March of that year. As I have said, within weeks of John being murdered, the names of the two gunmen were known to police investigating his murder. I believe their names were known because those gunmen and the mastermind behind the operation were secretly recorded in one of estate agent Joseph Fenton's bugged properties.

I believe someone didn't want to waste this opportunity to net a bigger fish in the deep and murky intelligence-gathering pond. So someone decided the murder of John Larmour was incidental collateral damage that could be easily added to the long list of lost lives and was nothing to worry about, the bigger picture being more important. I believe the decision was made to allow John's murder to proceed, and, after the operation, to arrest the "mastermind" and bring him in for questioning on some unrelated incident. The real reason for his arrest was to confront him with the secret recordings of himself in the bugged safe house, planning John's murder and subsequently celebrating his death along with the two gunmen. Damning, taped evidence that if acted upon, would put him in jail away from his family for a very long time. The spooks in MI5 and RUC Special Branch would have had the opportunity to offer the murder mastermind a deal that would turn him into one of their biggest and potentially most important assets within the IRA, right up there at the top table.

I believe the mastermind readily accepted the "get out of jail" card on offer. However, as is the right of any arrested person, including IRA members of course, he would have been entitled to have his lawyer of choice present during any questioning after arrest, especially at the infamous Castlereagh Holding Centre, commonly referred to by Republicans as "the Castlereagh Torture Centre".

So, to make it look right, was the mastermind allowed to telephone his lawyer, Pat Finucane? Did Finucane realise that his client had been in Castlereagh for a significant period of time before he was allowed to consult with him? Did Finucane suspect something wasn't quite right about his client's arrest that October in 1988? The lawyer would have known that MI5 and Special Branch often used arrests of IRA members as an opportunity to "turn" them.

Did his professional inquisitiveness start to cause concern for RUC Special Branch tout handlers? Were they afraid that Finucane might inadvertently get too close to the truth, that his client had been "turned"; that he was now a super tout? More generally, was Pat Finucane not just a thorn in the side of the police, for being able to represent his Republican clients (and others including Loyalists) successfully? But that in this instance, for proving that he was too good a lawyer to be fooled by the answers he was getting from Special Branch about his client's spurious arrest?

Perhaps Special Branch's coup in recruiting the mastermind as a super tout was becoming dangerously close to being unintentionally exposed by Pat Finucane? Perhaps the position of Super Tout was becoming so precarious that something radical had to be done to avoid his accidental exposure? Something as radical as his handlers involving themselves in the murder of his lawyer?

Loyalists must have rejoiced when they were provided with secret targeting information to facilitate the murder of someone they and some members of the RUC hated. Finucane would often be labelled "the IRA's lawyer" by those seeking justification for their actions. But in allegedly doing Special Branch's dirty work, had loyalists been unwittingly manipulated to solve a bigger problem, by the removal of a lawyer who was too good and was asking too many questions? And perhaps there were others, whose voices were on those bugged recordings; other IRA top table members, who Special Branch also had in their recruitment sights?

Over the years since Pat Finucane was killed, investigative journalists have speculated that the intelligence services allowed his planned murder to proceed, in order to protect an informer or informers they had within the loyalist Ulster Defence Association. There could be some element of truth in that hypothesis. However, I contend that Special Branch could have set Pat Finucane up for death to protect their new super tout – not within the UDA, but within the organisation he was accused of representing too successfully – the Provisional IRA. Is this the unpalatable truth that needs to be shielded from exposure in any independent Public inquiry – that Pat Finucane was murdered to protect the identity of an IRA godfather, who was selling information to the intelligence services?

Some might consider my hypothesis and interpretation of events to be absurd and fanciful; the paranoid thoughts of a grieving brother, whose judgement has been clouded by too many years of pain and despair. Some might think this is the stuff reserved for the well-thumbed pages of a fictional spy novel, in which imaginary informers and men in grey suits pull the strings that have us all dancing to whichever tune they choose.

Many will consider that, because I am a Protestant born on the Shankill Road, and the brother of an RUC member murdered by the IRA, I shouldn't give a damn about the murder of Pat Finucane – a person many armchair judges suggest was himself an IRA member, and who others have referred to as "the IRA's lawyer". Citing the fact that some of Pat Finucane's siblings were convicted IRA members and that he was IRA hunger striker, Bobby Sands' lawyer, they insist that he himself must have been an IRA member or sympathiser – and that he therefore deserved to be murdered.

From my standpoint, the simple reality is that I don't know if Pat Finucane was connected in any way to the IRA. I don't have the knowledge to make such a judgement, assumption or ill-informed allegation. I am really not that interested in what his background was. I am against violence and of the view that no one deserves to be murdered, no matter who they are. Behind every person murdered are family members, particularly children, who will be grieving the loss of someone they love and miss.

I care about the truth, however. The possibility that some faceless "men in grey suits" in MI5 or RUC Special Branch might have knowingly sanctioned the murders of my brother John and of Pat Finucane, and allowed the same fate to befall estate agent Joseph Fenton, all to protect a killer of their choosing, is quite simply, repugnant.

Perhaps the family of Pat Finucane might care to look at what I have set out here, and its timeline, and consider whether my interpretation is as far-fetched as it might seem at first glance. I hope I am correct in my interpretation. I hope the Finucane family's search for the truth is ultimately successful. I hope their efforts expose the IRA super tout I believe may be connected to Pat Finucane's murder. In doing so, they will help my own search for the truth and for the real reason as to why my brother John was murdered, and why no one has ever been brought to book for his killing.

Chapter Forty

The Estate Agent

Joseph Fenton was a self-employed estate agent during the 1980s in West Belfast, the heartland of the Belfast Brigade of the Provisional IRA. Towards the end of February 1989, just a few weeks after lawyer Patrick Finucane was murdered, Fenton was abducted. He was interrogated for two days by the infamous Internal Security Unit of the IRA, whose role was to seek out informers and deal with them. On the night of 26 February 1989, he was taken from the IRA interrogation house in Andersonstown, and executed. His body was dumped in an alleyway close to a local primary school; he had been shot a number of times in the head. Joseph Fenton was 35 years old.

The Internal Security Unit of the IRA was casually referred to as the "Nutting Squad", a title derived from local Belfast slang which describes someone's head as their "nut". Shooting alleged informers in the head appeared to be the preferred method of disposal for this unique squad of interrogators and killers, and in Fenton's case, they once again fulfilled their own brief.

Various reports from the IRA and local media sources at the time suggested that Joseph Fenton had broken during his interrogation by the Nutting Squad, and admitted to having worked as an informer for RUC Special Branch, perhaps from as early as 1981. His estate agency business had offered the perfect opportunity for him to provide the IRA with unoccupied properties in his portfolio, something the IRA was apparently all too willing to accept. Fenton was able to provide Republicans with safe houses for their on-the-run members and for private meetings between members of the IRA high command to plan attacks and general strategy. Unknown to the IRA, however, RUC Special Branch had access to those properties and had placed sophisticated listening and recording devices in the various rooms. It is therefore plausible that major PIRA operations, including the planned murders of security force members, were monitored and recorded, both in their preparation and follow-up stages.

It is difficult to say why Joseph Fenton – a young businessman with a wife and young children – became an informer. Was it, as has been suggested, a consequence of his allegedly transporting a one-off consignment of explosives across Belfast for the IRA? Did Special Branch seize or manufacture an opportunity to coerce Fenton into working for them, with the threat of being thrown into prison for a long time if he refused? Or was it because he disagreed with what the IRA was doing, and was therefore a willing participant in the murky and dangerous world of espionage? Or did Special Branch offer financial assistance to him to enable him to set up his estate agency business; did these inducements and his own dreams of commercial success cloud the judgement of an ambitious young man? No doubt his RUC Special Branch handlers could answer these and many other questions surrounding the life and death of Joseph Fenton. Unfortunately Fenton himself cannot.

Was the murder of my brother John in Barnam's planned, and afterwards, debriefed in one of those properties? Did members of the RUC Special Branch sit and drink tea and joke with each other in the safety of their base in Castlereagh or Police Headquarters in East Belfast, while they listened to and recorded the planning of the murder of one of their own RUC colleagues? I cannot prove it, but I firmly believe the answer to that question is an equally chilling "yes".

As I have suggested previously, I believe that the planned murder of my brother was allowed to proceed, to ensure that a number of Special Branch's high-ranking informers within the IRA would be protected, including at that stage Joseph Fenton. I believe too however that they eventually sacrificed the young estate agent, once they deemed that he had outlived his usefulness. There were bigger touts to protect.

As I have already stated, within weeks of my brother being murdered, I was told by members of the RUC who worked with John that reliable intelligence had been obtained, which confirmed the names of the two gunmen that night. I scoured the newspapers and listened to the local radio and television news channels during October and November 1988, expecting an announcement that the gunmen had been arrested, questioned and charged with John's murder. At the time I wasn't able to work out what was happening.

Looking back now in hindsight, it is easier to join up the dots. I believe the reliable intelligence referred to back in October 1988 was the Special Branch recordings obtained in Joseph Fenton's bugged properties. I believe Special Branch blocked the immediate arrest of the two known gunmen, because doing so would alert the IRA to the fact that a tout was operating in West Belfast. Special Branch knew the IRA would go hunting for that tout and the trail would eventually lead them to Joseph Fenton and his safe houses. Being able to continue their listening and recording of IRA operatives and their godfathers discussing future terror and destruction in bugged safe houses was more important than the life of another cop. John was expendable. I believe that Joseph Fenton didn't realise during October and November 1988 that he too would soon be considered disposable by his handlers in Special Branch, who had previously promised him so much.

As the team of Special Branch officers listened and recorded this senior Republican and respected IRA member confirming his organisational role in John's murder, and the details and names of those he instructed to carry out the murder, I believe that they decided the time was right for them to reel in this bigger fish.

I obviously don't know how Special Branch members perform the delicate task of approaching potential informers. Do they casually get into conversation with a potential tout in his local newsagent shop, and issue veiled threats about what they know about his personal life? Or do they have a vehicle checkpoint set up, where they stop him and give him the telephone number of a contact he should ring, coupled with a threat about his sexual preferences being exposed if he refuses? Recruiting touts is a skill they have perfected over many years. And the ultimate trick – of making touts disappear when they have outlived their usefulness – is something the masters of deception and deflection in Special Branch also have up their sleeves.

Christmas 1988 came and went. Many families didn't know what the New Year would bring. Did someone in Special Branch know exactly what it would bring to Joseph Fenton's door, when in January 1989 the RUC arrested the two IRA gunmen who allegedly killed my brother John? The suspects were brought to Castlereagh RUC Station, where they sat through three days of interrogation without speaking. During those three days, were they given just enough information from what was recorded in the safe houses to enable them to identify the source of the information, but not enough to charge them, because MI5 and Special Branch wanted them to be released and debriefed by the IRA? Did the spooks want the two alleged gunmen to tell their IRA masters that they were confronted with facts that could only have come from conversations they had had inside Joseph Fenton's supposed safe houses – locations that up until then the IRA had regarded as completely safe and secure? Was this a deliberate ploy on behalf of Special Branch to deflect attention away from the new super tout, and ensure that the Nutting Squad would decide to focus its attention on Joseph Fenton?

If so, their deception worked to perfection. Fenton was shot dead a few weeks later after being mercilessly interrogated and tortured. No one would have suspected there was a new super tout at the heart of the IRA.

In the period following his son's murder, the IRA presented Patrick Fenton with the written and taped confessions, which had been extracted from Joseph during his interrogation by the Nutting Squad. The grieving father subsequently issued a statement, saying he accepted the evidence provided to him by the IRA indicating that Joseph had been working as an informer. But Mr Fenton also angrily said that RUC pressure led directly to his son being murdered, and that Special Branch bore ultimate responsibility for his son being sucked into the murky world of informants, which resulted in his death. Meanwhile the IRA accused the RUC of lying in their statement shortly after Fenton's body was discovered in that West Belfast alleyway, in which they claimed that the young estate agent had had no connection with the security forces. The IRA said it was not prepared to disclose how it eventually detected that Joseph Fenton was an informant.

Do I have respect for informers? Truthfully, I don't know how to answer that question. Without them, no doubt many people alive today would otherwise be dead. Had my brother's life been saved by the work of an informer, I am sure I would have wanted to shake the hand of that person and thank them for having been brave enough to put their own life on the line to save John.

But someone like the super tout should not be honoured – he should be despised by all right-thinking people. He was not someone who made a conscious decision to turn away from violence and risk his own life in order to thwart the murderous actions of his comrades, nor was he driven by a desire to save lives. On the contrary, if media and security sources are to be believed, he relished his role as an IRA operator and killer, allegedly enjoying the fact that his handlers allowed him to continue his killing career. He was a real-life untouchable, with immunity from prosecution, and a "get-out-of-jail" amnesty letter neatly tucked into his back pocket for use at some future date if needed.

I am sure it will bring no comfort to his family when I say that, if Joseph

Fenton's true motivation in becoming an informer was a genuine desire to help stop the IRA killing his fellow human beings, then I admire him for having the courage to do what he did in pursuit of that goal. However this is probably not what they ever wanted to hear anyone to say about him. And I am sure that there may be families – of those he might have deliberately double-crossed to save his own skin, or those he might have been forced into exposing in order to protect his own identity – who might view him with a more jaundiced eye.

The simple truth is that I wish Joseph Fenton had not felt the need to become an informer; that he could have emigrated to Australia with his wife and family when he was accused of transporting explosives for the IRA back in 1981; that his father didn't have to "accept the evidence provided to him", that his son was a British agent.

§

I believe the killing of the Gibraltar Three in March 1988 started a murderous series of events that saw Michael Stone carry out his attack in Milltown that month, then Corporals Howes and Wood being murdered at the funeral of one of those killed by Stone, then my brother John being murdered in revenge for the killing of those in Gibraltar – all of which led ultimately to the orchestrated murders of Patrick Finucane and Joseph Fenton, and possibly the recruitment of the biggest super tout within the IRA. And it is my belief that there are former members of RUC Special Branch who know the truth.

After the murders of Patrick Finucane and Joseph Fenton in 1989, is it possible that the leaders of the IRA were still completely unaware of this super tout in their midst? Someone long considered one of the hawks within that organisation, who suddenly changed and supported Gerry Adams in his peace-building initiative. Did that not arouse suspicion and wonder – or are there those within Sinn Féin who have known of his existence and helped keep secret his identity and role as an informer?

Was his change of heart, from public hawk to dove, the price he had to finally pay for his betrayal and for their silence, to allow him to live out his old age? And why would they allow him to go unpunished? Are there those who need their own secrets to be guarded at all costs? Do they have skeletons in their own clandestine cupboards that need to be kept silent?

I'm sure Patrick Finucane's family wish their lives were not overshadowed by their campaign for justice and truth. Clearly Joseph Fenton's family wish he had not been sucked into the shadowy world of the informant. I'm sure his father wishes Joseph was still alive and enjoying a normal life on the other side of the world, just as I wish my brother was still alive and my mum and dad hadn't suffered his loss so greatly that they died prematurely from pure grief.

Instead, they and thousands of other forgotten victims of our Troubles share a small piece of this land we all call home and continue to fight over. A small piece of land where loved ones continue to lay flowers and shed their tears. And where too many secrets remain buried.

Chapter Forty-One

The Police Ombudsman

In September 2013 I met with Dr Michael Maguire, the Police Ombudsman for Northern Ireland (PONI), along with senior members from his own dedicated Historical Investigations Unit. I attended the meeting to discuss the fact that the then Chief Constable, Matt Baggott had failed to reply to the series of letters I had addressed to him.

I wasted no time in telling Dr Maguire that I was appalled that the Chief Constable had demonstrated such contempt for my legitimate anxieties, by simply transferring my concerns to PONI against my wishes. I stressed that I hadn't requested the Chief Constable's office to refer my dissatisfaction to the Police Ombudsman for Northern Ireland. I said to him that I reluctantly accepted that the Chief Constable's delaying tactic had succeeded, and that I was now left with no option but to agree to PONI officially investigating my concerns. I stressed to Dr Maguire however that I was only interested in PONI becoming involved if he was willing to fully investigate the allegation, that in 1988 certain members of RUC Special Branch could have prevented my brother being murdered by the IRA, and that subsequent Chief Constables, including Mr Baggott, might have knowingly prevented that truth being revealed, in order to ensure the continued protection of an IRA super tout.

Dr Maguire assured me that he was aware of the serious nature of my correspondence and allegations. He promised he would investigate my brother's murder fully and would do everything in his power to provide me with the truth which my family and I deserved.

At the conclusion of that initial meeting, a Family Liaison Officer was appointed. She assured me that the Ombudsman and his staff considered the families of victims as the most important people, and that she would be available at any time to discuss my concerns. We agreed that she would keep in contact with me every three months to update me on progress, even if that simply meant writing to explain that there had been no actual progress. At least being kept in the loop in this way would reassure me that things were still on track.

I suspected it would be many months – and perhaps years – before I received any kind of comprehensive report from Dr Maguire. And even at that point, I knew there would be every chance that the controlling fingerprints of the intelligence mandarins in Belfast and London would be fully in evidence in the pages of any such final report. I expected that the truth would be suppressed yet again.

§

Despite her assurances, after eight months I had yet to hear anything from the Family Liaison Officer, or indeed anyone at the PONI Office. So in early May 2014, I decided to telephone her for an update. During that brief telephone conversation, the Family Liaison Officer informed me that she had been promoted, and was no longer working on my brother's case. She named another member of staff, saying that they had been in contact with me. I had never heard of this person, and had never heard from him on behalf of PONI during the previous eight months. So much for the promise of keeping me informed, and the high priority being given to victims' family members.

A few hours later I received a telephone call from another staff member, informing me that he was now the investigator dealing with my brother's case. He invited me to visit him and another Family Liaison Officer, which I agreed to do, in the hope that they could update me on any progress.

On 8 May I met with them both as arranged. Once more, I left that meeting both thoroughly disillusioned and angry. To be greeted cheerily by them and assured that it was good for us all "to put names to faces" wasn't exactly the sum total of what I expected. The male staff member had gone on to assure me that he was actively "reading up" on my brother's case. This infuriated me even more. Eight months with no contact from my Family Liaison Officer, and this person was telling me that he was "reading up" on the case. It seemed like Groundhog Day. I was back to dealing with the same scenario I had experienced with the HET, as if the past eight months had never happened.

I asked them both if they could update me on any progress. Their simple answer was that there was no significant progress to report. I suggested that, as they were just familiarising themselves with the case, they obviously didn't know enough to provide me with any meaningful update, and asked if someone within PONI who could update me properly could attend the meeting. They reiterated that there was no "significant progress" to report from anyone within their organisation.

So, apart from "putting names to faces", my attendance at PONI that day, eight months later, was a waste of time. It left me totally disheartened, upset and frustrated. Sadly, these are emotions that the families of victims here have been experiencing over too many years. We have come to expect disappointment from those in authority, who seem to promise so much.

I fully appreciate of course how busy the Police Ombudsman and his staff are. I have the greatest respect for their efforts to deal with the many difficult and complex matters they face, and am aware of the enormous workload they must manage. In fact this was my main reason in the first instance for not wanting the Chief Constable to sideswipe my letters off his desk and onto that of the Ombudsman. I wasn't expecting some major development or substantial progress to be reported to me. But is it too much to ask that someone, tasked with dealing with such a sensitive issue and with grieving family members, could at least fulfil the promises they make?

I had thought my cooperation with PONI would be different. I had foolishly believed that the appalling HET experience and the callous treatment I received from the Chief Constable were not typical, and that someone did care how victims' family members felt; that we deserved better. Sadly, yet again, my recent experiences have shattered that illusion.

I appreciate some individuals employed there might look upon the work they do as just a job, and something from which they can easily "move on". For me and the thousands of victims and their family members in Northern Ireland, it is our lives and our pain they are dealing with. Do they not realise that some of us do not have the luxury of simply "moving on", until we get the truth. And that the way others deal with our anxiety and loss along that road to closure, truth and justice can make our journey more difficult.

The two new staff members were not to blame for my anger that day. They were able to appreciate and understand my genuine frustration and distress, and witnessed how raw the emotions of victims' family members can be, even many years later. They were in no doubt about how I felt. It was the same way I felt, when I was given that awful news more than 27 years ago, far away in Spain, that my brother had been murdered. It was the same way I felt when I buried my dad exactly one year after my brother, and when I buried my mum a few years after that. It is how I felt when I received that meaningless report from the HET, which told me nothing I didn't already know and concealed the truth of my brother John's murder; the same way I felt last year when Mr Baggott couldn't be bothered replying to my numerous letters. It is how I feel, when I listen to our highly paid MLAs talk about how important it is to deal with the past and how victims and their families deserve better; the same way I feel when I see their smiling faces, adorning lamp posts or on our doorsteps, as they scramble for our votes and then disappear, never to be heard from again. Does anyone in authority really, truthfully give a damn about victims and their families?

The following week I received a letter from the Ombudsman's Office, acknowledging my frustration and inviting me to arrange an appointment with Dr Maguire to discuss my concerns. I didn't bother replying. The thought of visiting his offices again, to be told once more how much they care about victims, was something I didn't want to contemplate. I had heard it so many times from so many people. Hopefully some day in the future, Dr Maguire will provide me with his report and it will contain the truth I seek. I think he will have a difficult task, trying to excavate any real truth from the cloying intelligence bog that holds all the secrets. Until then, I hope his staff care enough to at least keep me informed of any progress. I live in hope.

§

In May 2014, with the appointment of Mr Baggott's replacement, local man George Hamilton, I wrote an open letter to the new Chief Constable, which was published in some of the local newspapers. I also delivered a letter for George Hamilton to Police Headquarters on the day he took up his new position. After some pleasantries from one of his staff, I basically received the same old, well-rehearsed reply, to the effect that they considered the HET's review to have been "appropriate". That is not a word I would use to describe my protracted dealings with the HET. As far as I am concerned, that organisation was never fit for purpose. It appears that its role was simply to read through the old files, and come to the obvious conclusion that the original investigating team didn't do a proper job. Hardly a startling revelation or the closure victims' families expected from such a professional organisation. I am not surprised they are no longer in business.

Mr Hamilton's office also judged that there were no new evidential opportunities available regarding John's murder. How could there be, when the HET and subsequent Chief Constables have refused to pursue any of the potential evidential opportunities outlined in my correspondence to them? And once more, it was suggested to me by the new Chief Constable's administration that I might wish to contact the Police Ombudsman's office if I needed anything confirmed in that regard. So it looks as if like the deflection tactic adopted by Matt Baggott, of swiping everything across to the overloaded desk of Dr Maguire at PONI, is being used once again in my regard. Mr Hamilton's office didn't bother confirming if they had supplied the Police Ombudsman with the information he requested.

I had hoped George Hamilton might be different from all the rest.

Chapter Forty-Two

A Question of Truth

Frustrated with the lack of cooperation and honesty I had experienced from all the obvious official avenues available to victims and their families, I decided in 2014 that I had nothing to lose by making an approach to former IRA member, Tommy Gorman. This was the man who had contributed to Malachi O'Doherty's *Sunday Sequence* radio programme.

I made contact with Malachi O'Doherty, and asked him if he knew how I could get a letter delivered to Tommy Gorman. After carefully listening to my rationale for doing so, Malachi agreed to use a contact he had, in order to get my letter to the former IRA man. Here is what I wrote in that letter:

My name is George Larmour. I am 65 years old now, and like us all, I have no way of knowing how many years I have left in this life. But I am aware that the odds are certainly not getting any better!

My brother John was murdered by the IRA in my wife's ice cream parlour, Barnam's World of Ice Cream, on 11 October 1988. Since John was murdered, I have [been seeking] the truth. That started back in 1988, with the original RUC personnel tasked with investigating his murder. And in more recent years, with the Historical Enquiries Team, the PSNI Chief Constable, Matt Baggott and the Police Ombudsman for Northern Ireland, Dr Michael Maguire. All to no avail.

None of them, for whatever reason, seem interested in dealing with my requests for the truth, and my allegations that certain members of RUC Special Branch knowingly allowed my brother to be murdered, so that they could recruit and protect a super informer they wished to install at the highest level of the Provisional IRA in Belfast.

I appreciate my letter might appear strange, but I am keen

to know if you would be willing to meet with me at a time and location of your choosing. Distance is not a problem – I will travel myself to anywhere you decide. My reason for [wanting to meet you] is simply that I am aware of your publicly acknowledged participation in the IRA, and your apparent willingness to speak of your role without hesitation.

I listened to your participation in a *Sunday Sequence* radio programme a few years ago which was hosted by Malachi O'Doherty – hence my reason for contacting Malachi, in the hope that he might know how to deliver this letter to you. I hope he has been successful and [that] you accept it for what it is.

As I have already said, I have no way of knowing how much longer I have to live, but I made a promise to my mum and dad, who died prematurely of broken hearts back in 1989 and 1994, that I would try to find out the truth, or at least as much of it as made sense. I am not naïve enough to believe that now, many years later, someone is likely to see the inside of a courtroom, never mind a prison cell, for their part in the murder of my brother. There was a time when I expected justice. Those whose job it is to provide that justice have no desire to do so. I reluctantly accept that I will probably never get justice now after so many years. Personally, the truth is all that I desire . . .

. . . You have nothing to fear – either legally or physically – by agreeing to meet with me. I am documenting the murder of my brother in the context of the conflict we all lived through, and the effect it had on my family members. Whether it is worthy of publication is not important. I believe [what] is important is that all those who can tell their stories should do so, in the hope that others will learn from our actions and that something positive will come from those stories. [In the hope] that future generations will not need to tell such stories, because what happened in the past here will not happen again to them.

Although born on the Shankill Road and still living here in my pension years, I have never been connected in any way to any paramilitary organisation. My parents brought me up to respect people for who they are, rather than what religion they happen to be born into. Particularly my dad, whose lifelong friend was a man called John McCann from Andersonstown. A friendship that lasted until their deaths and was created when they both saved each other from drowning in the sea at Dunkirk as naïve and frightened 20-year-olds, who didn't give a damn about religion; who just wanted to live and get back home to Belfast.

I appreciate my timing could have been better, as I am sure you might be suspicious and cautious about my sudden request to meet with you, in the midst of the Boston Tapes débâcle. I have been considering making this approach for some time, and my timing is merely coincidental. I have no hidden agenda. I have no wish to record our conversation or have you provide me with any written responses.

I will not hide the fact that I disagree with your decision to join the IRA. Similarly, I have no problem with you disagreeing with my brother joining the RUC. We all make our own decisions in life. I wouldn't have joined the RUC or any Loyalist Paramilitary organisation. That's just me.

I am not looking for some sort of quasi-bereavement counselling from you to make me feel better. I am simply turning my attention to you, perhaps as a last resort, as someone I have known about [for a long time] in terms of a possible connection to the murder of my brother, and feel that if I am ever to get some element of the truth before I die, it might be from you. I've tried all the obvious avenues in my search for that elusive truth. I owe it to my brother, my mum and dad and to myself to at least put my questions to you – someone who has acknowledged his part in what happened here.

I hope you agree to [meet with me].

I included private contact details, so that he could reply directly to me, but Malachi also suggested that, if it helped, he would be happy to act as a go-between in the process. Within weeks, Malachi confirmed that he had managed to get my letter delivered to Tommy Gorman.

During 2014 Tommy Gorman had publicly confirmed that he had participated in the Boston College Oral History Project 14 years earlier, in which a number of former combatants of our conflict, both Republican and Loyalist, agreed to record their experiences. Those tapes were to be securely housed within Boston College in the US. Participants in this unique project were assured that their individual tapes would remain confidential and would not be released until after they were dead. However, in 2013 the Police Service of Northern Ireland were successful in their application to have some of these tapes handed over to them, as part of their investigation into the 1972 murder of mother of ten, Jean McConville, and the subsequent "disappearing" of her body.

Given this background, Malachi's contact felt that Tommy Gorman would naturally be cautious about entering into any discussion with me, because of how the Boston College Project guarantees had backfired on some of its participants, including himself.

§

I did not receive any direct reply from Tommy Gorman, so I quickly accepted that my letter would not have the outcome I had hoped for – something that was confirmed on 14 January 2015. Unknown to me, Malachi had that day spoken directly with Gorman on another matter. He said he did not get into discussion about the specific content of my letter, but that he had asked Gorman if there was any chance he would ever agree to meet with me. Malachi confirmed to me that, unfortunately, he was adamant that he did not wish to do so.

I was disappointed. Over the past 27 years I had on many occasions publicly and privately demanded that the RUC, PSNI, HET and Police Ombudsman pursue every opportunity to properly investigate my brother's murder and those involved. But that was not the motivation behind my carefully composed letter to Tommy Gorman. I had hoped he would be convinced that I was genuine in my approach, that I did not have any hidden agenda and that all I wanted was the opportunity to talk to him about my quest for the truth. Most of all, I wanted him to believe that he had nothing to fear from speaking to me.

Over many years, Gorman has shown that he is willing to talk openly about his past to documentary-makers and writers. He has participated in cross-community discussions with former Loyalist prisoners. As has been discussed in an earlier chapter, when in 2013 Sinn Féin President, Gerry Adams refused to meet with the parents of Stephen Melrose, who had been killed by the IRA in Holland, Tommy Gorman invited them to his home in Donegal. He spoke to them at length about his IRA past and the inexcusable murder of their innocent son. He had then participated in the *Sunday Sequence* radio programme hosted by Malachi. So I wasn't asking him to do something he had never done before.

If he had agreed to meet with me, I would have welcomed the opportunity to ask him if what he had said in his *Sunday Sequence* radio interview about his IRA past and the fact that he "regretted every minute of it" extended to the murder of my brother John, who was a member of the RUC.

I would have spoken to him about his public acknowledgment that he had brothers who were members of the British Army and Merchant Navy, and indeed that one of his brothers was also a member of the RUC. I would have been keen to ask him, if that brother had been murdered by the IRA because of his RUC role, would he, Tommy Gorman, have agreed with him being killed simply for his choice of career? I would have asked him if he believed what had been reported in local Sunday newspapers, that a senior member (not him) of the PIRA unit he belonged to in West Belfast was allegedly recruited as a super tout after the murder of my brother. I would have asked him if he considered the murder of my brother John to be a fitting tribute to the memory of the Gibraltar Three and particularly to his friend Dan McCann.

I would have asked him, if he had the chance to speak to them today, what he would say to my mum and dad, who died prematurely from grief as a result of their son having been murdered by the IRA. I would have asked him what he would say to my brother John, if he had the chance to speak to him today.

Chapter Forty-Three

Turning Another Page

There comes a time when you have to choose between turning another page and closing the book. I suppose I have arrived at that crossroads in my search for the truth.

It is hard to believe it's been 27 years since October 1988, when I last spoke to my brother. It has been a long and difficult time. I'm beginning to feel every one of my pensioner years now. The hair is greyer; the aches and pains multiply. How little we knew as kids about how things would turn out, John!

I must confess, while I don't do it so much now, many times during those years I would drive out to the cemetery in Ballyclare to visit your grave. If it was raining, as it often was, I would just sit in the car and stare out the window at your headstone and get lost in my memories.

The great times we had every year, down at the little summer cottage Mum and Dad rented near Doagh. Those warm summer days working at Robson's farm. You were always braver than I was, the first to try anything new. But I suppose that's how big brothers are meant to be. Messing about on tractors, herding in cows for milking, mucking out pig byres, tumbling down hay-bale stacks, drinking crystal-clear water from the stream in our cupped hands, catching trout from the Six Mile River – even picking potatoes, back-breaking work, was great fun for us city kids. Wonderful childhood memories. I miss those days.

Of course they were never going to last. With age comes an inevitable transition, and the day arrived when you were too old for all that nonsense. During your teenage years, no longer wanting me hanging around, you had your own mates, Chubby Checker's new dance craze 'The Twist' to perfect and girls to impress – while I still had my slapped-arse cowboys to deal with.

What a difference a few years can make. Teenage years stole our innocence and separated us. You left school, trained to be an electrician and became a weekend goal-scoring maestro on the football pitches of some of the local clubs. I stayed on at school and discovered Dusty Springfield and the

Beatles. All too quickly we were adults, husbands, fathers … and then you were gone.

With the view of your headstone no longer clear through the steamed-up car window, I would drive out of the cemetery, wishing we could go for a pint and catch up on all those times together. I miss you, John.

I'm sorry I didn't find the truth for you. I have tried. I've wasted too many years, chasing shadows and liars. Like all victims and their families, I shouldn't have had to carry out my own investigations. We expect the police to do that, but they don't always do their job. We hear about the need for transparency when dealing with our Troubles past: there is none. We hear how victims and their families deserve justice: there isn't any.

"To the living we owe respect, but to the dead we owe only the truth." Those words of wisdom from Voltaire in the opening pages of this book reflect my own experience over the past 27 years, and will be deeply understood by many victims' families. Too many have been shown very little respect by those in authority, who say they care. Most of our Troubles' dead are still owed the truth. Maybe one day, someone will find the courage to do what is right and admit the truth; in doing so, they will cleanse their consciences about the part they played in your murder and its cover-up.

Perhaps this is where normal life starts again for me, before it's too late, and it will take me on whatever journey it has in store. I'll live out the rest of my existence here, where it started. This little piece of land that has so many names – from its official title, "Northern Ireland", to the abbreviated "the North", to "the Six Counties" or "the Province", depending on the perspective of the speaker. But it's a place that those lucky enough to have taken their first breath here, who have felt its magic and heard its heartbeat, can call home.

Possibly one day I will finally find the pot of gold at the end of that elusive rainbow of truth; I will uncover the full story that I, like so many other bereaved relatives, have been rummaging for in the dust-covered files of the forgotten dead. We have become used to glimpsing, every few years, that arc of hope in the skies above our troubled land. But for so many of us, it was just a fleeting glimmer of the much-promised justice we all long for, one which ultimately disappeared into the gloom of another tear-stained pillow of despondency and frustration.

The strength and determination of others, who have campaigned publicly and tirelessly for justice for the murders of their own loved ones, taken alongside my own less vocal efforts over the past 27 years, have often left me humbled. Ordinary people, who were hurled into the spotlight and often abused for simply wanting to seek justice for those they loved – a sister or brother, a mum or dad, a spouse or even, tragically in some cases, a child. Collateral casualties in our grotesque, grubby sectarian conflict, which saw some people deliberately chosen and ambushed by human exterminators slaking their tit-for-tat craving for slaughter.

I think now of Ann Travers, missing her beautiful sister, Mary; Colin and Wendy Parry, missing their 12-year-old, Everton-supporter son, Tim; the McCartney sisters, missing their brother, Robert; Geraldine Finucane, missing her husband, Pat; Alan McBride, missing his wife, Sharon and his father-in-law; Desmond, of the McConville children, missing their mum, Jean, so callously killed and "disappeared"; and my nephew Gavin, missing his dad, and who will never give up seeking truth and justice. Too many names. Please forgive me for not mentioning them all.

And too many places. Claudy, Enniskillen, Dublin, Monaghan, Omagh, Kingsmill, Shankill, Ballymurphy, La Mon, Greysteel, Darkley. Each place name is a reminder of families still suffering the pain of personal loss. Again, please forgive me for not mentioning them all.

It is now over two years since my legitimate questions were deliberately ignored by former Chief Constable, Matt Baggott and, against my wishes, off-loaded to the Police Ombudsman's office. I am still waiting for answers. Financial cutbacks have ensured Dr Maguire's already burdened desk will not be cleared any time soon. He does however keep me regularly updated now, and I appreciate his genuine understanding of how victims' families feel. He seems to care. Here's hoping he has the courage to fulfil the promises he made to me in his office that day in September 2013. I am ever hopeful – and yet I very much doubt it. Even if he uncovers the truth, I expect he might be prevented from revealing it by other, more powerful government agencies who need to ensure at all costs that the facts remain hidden.

As I look back on the past 27 years, I have arrived at the conclusion that victims and their families are of no consequence to those in government. We are not important – just a bloody nuisance. And all the patronising words and "victim-centred" phrases we have heard from government and politicians over so many years are just that: words and clever soundbites that bring no comfort and no answers. What a truly duplicitous and wretched shower of hypocrites we foolishly voted for on all sides!

For years after John was murdered, I dreaded the anniversary of his death, 11 October. As well as John's murder, I would remember my uncle Jackie going missing on that date back in 1960, Mr Hasty being killed on that date in 1974, and my dad being buried on that same day in 1989. Each time another 11 October passed without incident, I said a silent "thank you" – it was a good day.

No doubt the family of RUC Constable Victor Arbuckle also view that date with such feelings. He was the first policeman to be killed during the Northern Ireland Troubles. Married with a young son, he was just 29 when, on 11 October 1969, he was shot and killed during a Loyalist riot on Belfast's Shankill Road.

I hope my own day of final departure, when it comes, will be many years away. There are too many things still to do, places to see. I'm sure there will be many more people I have still to meet in the time I have left, who will touch my life. I hope most of them are kind and that their influence doesn't hurt me or those I love. Former US First Lady, Eleanor Roosevelt wrote the following lines: "Many people will walk in and out of your life, but true friends will leave footprints in your heart." Sadly, some people came into our family's life in 1988 and left behind only debris, blood and sorrow.

My story is of course only one of many. Over 3,500 people died in our recent Troubles. Behind each statistic is a family still hurting. Thousands more were horribly maimed, each one of them with a story to tell. They should never be forgotten. For many it will be painful, but we all deserve the truth.

Many of you, having read my story, will conclude that since I have not found that truth, it was all a waste of time. Probably true – but since those tasked with establishing the truth have refused to do so, what else could I do? Many of you will suggest that I haven't substantiated a number of my allegations. Again, I will not argue with your interpretation. Only those who know the truth can challenge or confirm my claims, and they have refused to do so. So many families have been left waiting for answers. In the absence of the elusive truth, we grasp at anything that might make sense of the madness we are left to endure.

I believe what I have written to be true. If anyone reading my story knows the real facts, I hope one day they find the courage to tell me them. Telling our stories would seem to be the only avenue left to many of us, as the years pass and our loved ones are in danger of being forgotten. And as others try to rewrite history in an attempt to sanitise the part they willingly played in cold-blooded murder.

All I can do is thank you for taking the time to walk with me this far in my search for that truth. I'm sure there were times you wished you hadn't bothered. I am certain there have been times – probably too many – when I have sounded miserable and self-obsessed, as if I am the only person in the world who has ever experienced grief or tragedy or heartbreak. The long trek probably depressed more than uplifted you. Maybe it was a journey you wished you hadn't started. I don't expect everyone to be sympathetic to my story, but I hope I have at least made you think about it.

I can only apologise if my story didn't live up to your expectations. When I started, I didn't know what I would write. Dealing with murder is something you can't prepare for. There's no definitive handbook, telling you how you should cope. It brings a grief that takes you, smothers you in a heavy shroud of desolation, changes you and sometimes moulds you into something you don't always like. I just hope you never have to learn the best way to handle such grief: sadly, you'll realise there simply isn't one. If you've had to deal with the murder of someone you loved, you will know what I mean. If you find yourself unexpectedly in that place sometime in the future, I hope these words of mine might help in some way.

I suppose this is the chapter many of you will have been looking forward to – the point where you can hope for that feel-good moment to make life all better again. The part of my story where I say all the right things and forgive the people who killed my brother. Just like in the movies, when at the end of the film James Stewart gives that lasting smile to the camera, and you just know there is always going to be a happy ending.

I wish I was that sort of person. But I'm not. I'm unable to manage the gesture of Christian charity offered by Gordon Wilson, who forgave the IRA killers of his 20-year-old daughter, Marie, in the Enniskillen bomb on Remembrance Day in 1987. His account, of lying in the debris holding her hand as she died, captures, for me, one of the most poignant moments in all the atrocities of our Troubles.

As much as I have tried, I just can't wipe away the past 27 years that easily. Why would I want to forgive those gunmen and their masters for killing my brother, for "killing" my mum and dad? For destroying so many lives. For ruining so many birthdays and Christmas days. For murdering innocence. And in any case, I don't have the authority to forgive them. That right ultimately belongs to my brother, and whatever God his killers believe in – if any.

The two gunmen who pulled the triggers that night have never been convicted of my brother's murder. Super Tout probably still enjoys the protection of his police handlers, confident he will never see the inside of a courtroom or prison cell. He no doubt has his thirty pieces of silver and his own exclusive amnesty scroll securely tucked away in the retirement safe house provided by his government paymasters.

Those Special Branch officers, John's back-stabbing RUC colleagues, who allegedly listened as killers planned his murder, are probably enjoying their retirement too, picking up their Brutus pensions for a job well done, staying silent to protect their touts and themselves.

What happened to that scrap of paper I found in John's car back in 1988 – the one with the Ford Sierra car registration number written on it? A car that the senior detective in Donegall Pass police station told me belonged to one of the people I picked out in the mugshot folders, not long after John's death.

Well, in 2008 as part of my co-operation with the Historical Enquiries Team, I asked that same question and in response, my HET contact, David Brown, showed me a sealed, see-through police evidence bag. In it was a white envelope with a car registration number and the word "Sierra" written on it. He informed me that this is what he had retrieved from the official police evidence storage files. He also said there was a report in the file indicating that the car registration number written on the envelope did not match the car owned by the person I had picked out; that one of the digits in the number was not the same.

So, 20 years after I handed in a scrap of paper with the word "Sierra" and a car registration number written on it, one which was confirmed on that same night by a leading detective as being identical to the registration number of a Ford Sierra car owned by the person I picked out, that scrap of paper had mysteriously turned itself into an envelope, on which was transcribed the same registration number, except with one digit altered.

Furious, I told David Brown that I believed someone had intentionally destroyed the original scrap of paper I handed in, and replaced it with an envelope that had that deliberately altered registration number on it. He immediately asked me if I might be mistaken, which angered me even more. I told him I was certain that I had found a scrap of paper, not an envelope, in John's car in 1988. That I had handed in that scrap of paper to Donegall Pass police station. That I had been told by the detective there that the number on it was identical to the registration number of the Ford Sierra car owned by the person I picked out from the mugshots – not that it almost matched.

His response was that he could only review the evidence available to him as part of his cold case review into John's murder and that the envelope was all he could find in the evidence files. He essentially told me that with the passage of time, it was impossible for him to pursue that particular line of enquiry now. I asked him if he could tell me if my fingerprints were found on the envelope. He confirmed that they had tested it and found some fingerprints, but that they were not mine. I then asked him if the writing on the envelope matched John's handwriting. He confirmed that, having done a forensic comparison, they had found that it didn't.

This convinced me even more that the scrap of paper I had originally handed in had been intentionally destroyed, and that the evidence had been tampered with. Why did someone need to do that? Who decided that this piece of evidence needed to be altered? Did someone need to be protected? Why? More questions added to the already long list of unanswered questions surrounding John's murder. David Brown reiterated that he could not pursue this potential evidential line of enquiry.

All the "suspects" can sleep peacefully in their beds. No one is going to knock on their doors and bring them to justice. This place is a land of deceit. No one dares lance the boil of our Troubles past. No one will release the putrid pus of truth, spilling out the names of those who pulled the triggers and the strings, played God and decided who should live or die.

They're all still out there in society, walking freely and getting on with their lives as they have done ever since that cold, dark night on 11 October 1988. They are hugging their families, laughing and presumably proud of their achievements. I don't anticipate the gunmen will apologise to me. They doubtless don't give a damn how I feel. They believed that killing my brother was the right thing to do. They presumably had the justification they needed, and exacting revenge for their own comrades killed in Gibraltar was all that mattered.

There have been times when I have hated my brother's killers; times when anger has almost changed me from the person my parents brought me up to be. Someone who accepted where he was born, on the Protestant Shankill Road, as something to be proud of, but not as something that should make him hate others, who were born Catholics on the nearby Falls Road or anywhere else on this little plot of land.

But although I will never forgive, I also see the futility of revenge. Often I have found myself in conversation with people who had never experienced murder. Many put forward the simplistic opinion that if they couldn't get proper justice, they would resort to the next best option – revenge. Whenever I hear that word, I am always reminded of the proverb attributed to the famous Chinese thinker and social philosopher, Confucius: "Before you embark on a journey of revenge, dig two graves." Too many people here have literally dug their own graves in their pursuit of revenge. And for those who survived their bloody journey of retaliation, their satisfaction has been short-lived. Killing someone else didn't bring them peace and closure – just depression and nightmares in the living tomb they have dug for themselves.

As innocent children, we started life swimming together in that chlorinated pool in the Falls Baths – or, in my case, splashed about, trying to swim. I never learned that important lesson. And some of us never learn even more important lessons. Some of us end up drowning in our own hatred of one another.

"Make sure ya don't swalley the water," my childhood saviour told me that day in the pool so many years ago. Wise words. Sadly, some ingested more than that polluted water. They swallowed too easily what others told them; they gulped down entrenched, bitter sectarian beliefs, which swamped their once innocent minds and turned them into the next bunch of killers.

I'm sure the two gunmen know what it is like to carry the coffins of their comrades-in-arms, but I hope they never have to carry the coffin of one of their own children. That's not the way it is supposed to work – parents shouldn't have to bury their children. But that's the heavy burden my dad had to bear on his weary, sunken shoulders the last time he saw his son, killed by someone with a heart filled with hate.

My story will continue. I don't think I will ever completely close the book on my search for the truth, but for now, I will stop turning the pages and enjoy what's left of my life. For me, it is the innocence of the laughing children, like little Sarah Longley, who loved our Honey Bear and Blue Surprise ice creams, which sums up the futility of what the IRA gunmen really achieved that night in Barnam's.

They killed the ice cream man.

Epilogue

It is the evening of 23 March 2015, and I find myself sitting among dignitaries from the world of the arts and media in the grand surroundings of the Ulster Hall in Belfast. I feel out of place among such well-known faces as the then Lord Mayor of Belfast, Nichola Mallon, local sporting legend, Dame Mary Peters, writers such as Glenn Patterson and Malachi O'Doherty, playwright Martin Lynch and many more that are unknown to me. But I am honoured to have received an invitation to this illustrious gathering, at which award-winning poet Michael Longley will have bestowed upon him the Freedom of the City of Belfast for his outstanding contribution to the arts and his poetry penned over more than five decades.

Another local poet, Frank Ormsby takes to the stage to speak about Michael and, in commenting on his many poems, he reflects on one in particular, "The Ice-Cream Man". I overhear the lady sitting next to me whispering to her partner that this is also one of her favourites.

Later in the proceedings the President of Ireland, Michael D Higgins, who has travelled north with his wife to be part of this civic honouring of his fellow poet and friend, is invited onto the stage to pay tribute to Michael Longley, and sum up his contribution to literature and the arts. He describes him as, "a remarkable man", noting that, "his poems speak for themselves; eloquent, precise and passionate, large-hearted, intelligent and above all, humane". He refers to "The Ice-Cream Man" as one of the most powerful examples of that humane quality Michael Longley so carefully weaves into his poems.

When the ceremony is over and the audience starts to mingle before leaving, I spot Michael Longley's daughter, Sarah, holding the hand of one of her children. The last time I saw her was when she was that young girl who dithered every week, as she pondered which ice cream she would spend her pocket money on in Barnam's. I cautiously introduce myself and remark that it has been a long time since my wife and I served her ice cream.

Sarah instantly knows who I am, and says her dad will be so pleased that I have come to the ceremony. She begins to reflect on that week in 1988, and I am surprised how emotional I feel. Thankfully, we are interrupted by another well-wisher who also hasn't seen her for many years. I am glad of the interruption, as I am finding this brief encounter overwhelming.

On stage, Michael Longley is now surrounded by journalists holding notepads and microphones, each one hoping to get the best quote from this new Freeman of the City. His attention is focused on answering their questions but as I politely go to shake his hand, we instead embrace each other as if we were brothers. I thank him for allowing me to be a part of his special night and again thank him for writing "The Ice-Cream Man". I find it humbling that Michael Longley is thanking me and saying he wished he had never had to write the poem.

On my way out of the building, I come face-to-face with Michael D Higgins, who is surrounded by his personal security staff. He instinctively shakes my hand, something he obviously does on such occasions, whether he knows the person he is greeting or not. I thank him for mentioning "The Ice-Cream Man" during his speech. He replies that it is one of his favourite poems. I tell him I am the Ice Cream Man's brother, and the President of Ireland hugs me. He says the murder of my brother was a terrible thing, and that Michael Longley's simple yet powerful elegy will ensure that John will never be forgotten.

As I leave the building and make my way home, along Bedford Street, I remember a novel I read some years ago, *The Twelve*, by local author Stuart Neville. It is a story about a former IRA hitman, Gerry Fegan, who is haunted by the ghosts of twelve people he killed during the Troubles. I find myself thinking that my own ghosts were in the Ulster Hall with me earlier that evening, and that they were all smiling. My mum and dad, John McCann, Jimmy Hasty and of course John, my brother.

I also wish you hadn't had to write "The Ice-Cream Man", Mr Longley, and that my brother was still alive – but I thank you for having done so and for ensuring, as Michael D Higgins said, that my brother John will never be forgotten.

Acknowledgements

I'd like to thank everyone who helped me tell my story. Many of you would prefer to remain nameless for your own reasons, but you know who you are. You will be forever in my thoughts, as you spend the rest of your own lives wondering how it ended up the way it did.

To Malcolm Johnston and everyone at Colourpoint Books, for believing in my story, and numerous journalists, who listened and encouraged me to keep digging and demanding the truth. But in particular, my thanks go to local journalist, broadcaster and author, Malachi O'Doherty for his help and guidance and always being there at the other end of a text or email or on the other side of a coffee table, steering me in the right direction. And of course to my editor, Susan Feldstein who, with her in-built sensitivity and attention to detail, brought a clarity to my story that allowed my voice to come through on every page.

To Michael Longley, for his kind words and Christmas cards over the years, and for penning his wonderful elegy to my brother John.

To Margaret (Mrs Hasty), for allowing me to include her own heartache in my story, and for being a friend.

And of course the biggest "thank you" is for my wife, Sadie and daughters, Ali and Em, who have had to put up with a grumpy husband and dad, as I persisted in my search for the truth. I couldn't have completed this without you – I love you so much.

Index

Abernethy, Colin 10, 113, 118, 121, 122, 153

Adams, Gerry 60, 88, 91, 132, 135, 138, 140, 152, 154, 173, 183

Ahern, Bertie (Former Taoiseach) 89

Andersonstown Road 65, 94, 169, 182

An Phoblacht 21, 61, 112

Arbuckle, Constable Victor 188

Austin, Joe 59

Baggott, Matt (Former Chief Constable, PSNI) 150, 156–159, 160–163, 175, 177, 178, 180, 187

Ballard, Brian 74

Baxter, Senior Aircraftman John 134

Belfast Telegraph 5, 62, 74, 76, 88, 90, 105, 130

Belgium 100, 101, 108, 109, 135, 136

Blair, Tony (Former Prime Minister) 88–90

Boston College Oral History Project 182–183

Bradley, Denis 105–106

Brady, Kevin (Caoimhin MacBradaigh) 61, 94, 95

Brown, David (Lead Senior Investigating Officer, HET) 112–113, 129, 151, 152, 156, 159, 161, 190–191

Browning 9 mm 19, 21, 60, 93–95, 97–99, 100, 135, 136, 143, 145

Butler, Lance Corporal Roy 95, 99

Cameron, David (Prime Minister) 164

Castlereagh RUC Station 153, 157, 166, 170, 171

Coulthart, Ross 132, 136–138

Cox, David (Head of the HET) 103, 113–115, 150

Crane, Prof Jack 85–87

DNA 99, 101, 107–111, 112, 121, 128, 129, 130

Davey, John Joe 123

Dillon-Lee, Major Mike 95, 135

Donaldson, Denis 153

Donegall Pass Police Station 22, 54, 55, 190, 191

Dunkirk 9, 36, 64–65, 84, 182

Duquesa de Espana (Spain) 23

Eames/Bradley Consultative Group on the Past 105–106

Eames, Lord Robin 105–106

Falls Baths 12, 45, 192

Falls Road 11, 12, 45, 192

Farrell, Mairéad 58–59, 94, 145

Fenton, Joseph 153, 156, 157–158, 166, 168, 169–174

Ferguson, Constable Michael 141–151, 163

Finaghy 100, 121

Finucane, Geraldine 164, 187

Finucane, Patrick 164–168, 169, 173, 174

Forensic Science Laboratory 108, 109, 114, 116, 120, 128, 129

Forensic Science Service 109, 116

Germany 95, 97, 98–99, 132, 134, 135, 136

Gibraltar 58–59, 60, 94, 145, 166, 173, 191

Gibraltar Three 58–59, 60, 61, 94, 141, 173, 184

Gorman, Tommy 138, 139–141, 180, 182, 183–184

Hamilton, George (Chief Constable, PSNI) 99, 178–179

Harland and Wolff shipyard 43

Harte, Gerard 95, 135

Hasty, Jimmy 9, 76–79, 80–84, 188, 194

Hasty, Margaret 80–84, 195

Herdman, Terry 139, 140

Hermon, Sir John (Former Chief Constable, RUC) 33–35

Hick, Sean 95, 135

Higgins, Michael D (President of Ireland) 193, 194

Historical Enquiries Team (HET) 96–99, 100–101, 102–104, 106, 108–111, 112–115, 116, 118, 119, 120–123, 127, 128, 129–130, 136, 142, 144, 148, 149–151, 152, 155, 156, 158, 159, 161, 176, 177, 178, 179, 180, 183, 190

Holland (the Netherlands) 97, 100, 118, 122, 132–133, 135, 136, 137, 138, 141, 183

Howes, Corporal David 94–95, 99, 173

Hughes, Paul 95, 135

INLA 140

IRA (Irish Republican Army) 21, 24, 25, 42, 45–46, 54, 58–59, 61, 82, 90–91, 94–95, 97, 99, 100, 101, 104, 105, 111, 112, 118, 119, 124, 125, 132–135, 137, 138, 139–140, 141, 142, 143, 145–147, 148, 152–155, 156–158, 166–168, 169–173, 175, 180–182, 183–184, 189, 192, 194

IRA Army Council 132, 152, 154, 158

Islania, Maheshkumar 134–135

Islania, Nivruti Mahesh 134–135

Islania, Smita 134–135

Larmour, Gavin (nephew) 69, 98, 100, 187

Larmour, Jean (sister) 9, 38

Larmour, John (father) 9, 11, 25, 26, 28, 36–40, 41, 42, 45, 56, 64–65, 67, 79, 84, 105, 113, 150, 174, 177, 181, 182, 184, 185, 188, 189, 192, 194

Larmour, Rosetta (mother) 9, 24, 26, 28, 38, 42–43, 45–46, 65, 66, 67, 71, 72, 73–75, 79, 80, 84, 105, 113, 140, 150, 174, 178, 181, 182, 184, 185, 189, 194

Lisburn Road 15, 16, 21, 53, 54, 57, 72, 74, 78, 147

Longley, Michael 9, 71–75, 193–194, 195

Longley, Sarah 72, 73, 138, 192, 193–194

MI5 152, 153, 154, 155, 156, 158, 165, 166, 168, 171

Maguire, Donna 95, 135, 137

Maguire, Dr Michael (Police Ombudsman) 175, 176, 178, 179, 180, 187

Melrose, Beverley 136, 138, 139

Melrose, Stephen 100, 113, 118, 122, 132–135, 136–138, 141, 183

Melrose, Roy 136, 138

Milltown Cemetery 60–61, 94, 95, 112, 116, 118, 119, 121, 122, 123, 173

Murray, John 'Minto' 61, 121, 122

McCabe, Gerry (Garda) 89

McCann, Daniel 58–59, 94, 141, 145, 184

McCann, John 9, 64–65, 65, 84, 182, 194

McCartney, Robert 90, 91, 92, 184

McConville, Jean 183, 187

McErlean, Thomas 61

McGuinness, Martin (deputy First Minister) 60, 91, 102, 103–104, 132, 154

News Letter 102, 104

Night Life 5

None Shall Divide Us, Michael Stone (Blake Publishing, 1992) 122

NORAID (Irish Northern Aid Committee) 125

Northumberland Street 11

Orange Order 16, 152, 154

Orde, Sir Hugh (Former Chief Constable, PSNI) 103

O'Doherty, Malachi 139, 140, 180–184, 193, 195

Paisley, Ian 89

Park Shopping Centre 95

Police Ombudsman for Northern Ireland (PONI) 143, 161–163, 175–179, 180, 183, 187

Police Service of Northern Ireland (PSNI) 96, 99, 110, 113, 114, 118, 120, 149, 150, 151, 160–163, 180, 183

Reagan, Ronald (President) 124–127

Reid, Senior Aircraftman John 134

Reid, Stanley 62–63

Roermond (Holland) 100, 122, 132–134, 137

RUC (Royal Ulster Constabulary) 21, 25, 33–35, 42, 54–56, 59, 78–79, 90, 91, 98, 99, 100, 105, 110, 112, 113, 115, 116, 117, 118, 119–122, 124, 125–127, 130, 136, 138, 140, 141, 142, 143, 144, 145–146, 147, 149, 150, 152, 153, 154–155, 156, 157, 158, 163, 166, 167, 168, 169, 170, 171, 172, 173, 175, 180, 182, 183, 184, 188, 190

Ruger .357 Magnum revolver 18, 21, 61, 100–101, 108–111, 112–115, 116–118, 119–123, 124–127, 128–131, 135, 136, 141, 142, 153

SAS 58–59, 145

Savage, Sean 58–59, 94, 145

Scappaticci, Freddie 153, 158

Shankill Road 5, 11, 12, 43, 63, 64, 76, 79, 168, 181, 187, 188, 191

Shinner, Ian 134

Sinn Féin 59, 60, 91, 104, 123, 132, 135, 140, 152, 154, 173, 183

Spanos, Nick 100, 113, 118, 122, 132, 134, 135, 136, 138

Special Branch 153, 155, 156, 158, 165–167, 168, 169–173, 175, 180, 190

"Stakeknife" 158

Stone, Michael 60–61, 94, 95, 112, 116, 118, 119, 121, 122, 123, 173

Stormont 104, 132, 141, 154

Sunday Life 153–154, 155, 156

Sunday Sequence 139, 140, 141, 180, 181, 184

Sunday Tribune 137

Sunday World 152–153, 154, 156

Super Tout 152–155, 157, 158, 159, 167, 168, 172, 173, 175, 180, 184, 190

Suspect 7 144–146, 147–148, 149–150, 151, 152, 158–159

Thatcher, Margaret (Prime Minister) 59, 125, 126, 127, 165

"The Ice-Cream Man", Michael Longley (Jonathan Cape, 1998) 9, 14, 71–75, 193, 194

The Twelve, Stuart Neville (Vintage, 2010) 194

Travers, Ann 187

Ulster Defence Association (UDA) 140, 153, 167

Ulster Defence Regiment (UDR) 143, 95

Ulster Volunteer Force (UVF) 140, 153

Voltaire 186

Waterstones Bookshop 71–75

We Wrecked the Place, Jonathan Stevenson (The Free Press, 1997) 140–141

Wilson, Gordon 189

Wood, Corporal Derek 93–95, 97–99, 136, 173

Woodvale Park 11